THE LITERATURE OF
DEATH AND DYING

Suicide
and Homicide

Andrew F. Henry

and James F. Short, Jr.

ARNO PRESS

A New York Times Company

New York / 1977

Reprint Edition 1977 by Arno Press Inc.

Copyright 1954 by The Free Press,
  A Corporation

This edition is reprinted by arrangement
  with The Free Press, A Division of
  Macmillan Publishing Company, Inc.

Reprinted from a copy in
  The Pennsylvania State Library

THE LITERATURE OF DEATH AND DYING
ISBN for complete set: 0-405-09550-3
See last pages of this volume for titles.

Manufactured in the United States of America

———◆———

Library of Congress Cataloging in Publication Data

Henry, Andrew F
    Suicide and homicide.

    (The Literature of death and dying)
    Reprint of the ed. published by Free Press, Glencoe,
Ill.
    Bibliography: p.
    1. Suicide--United States. 2. Homicide--United
States. I. Short, James F., joint author. II. Title.
III. Series.
[HV6548.U5H45 1977]   362.2   76-19575
ISBN 0-405-09573-2

Suicide
and Homicide

SOME ECONOMIC, SOCIOLOGICAL AND PSYCHOLOGICAL
ASPECTS OF AGGRESSION

by Andrew F. Henry HARVARD UNIVERSITY

and James F. Short, Jr. STATE COLLEGE OF WASHINGTON

THE FREE PRESS, GLENCOE, ILLINOIS

To

Mary and Kelma

CONTENTS

I. Introductory Statement   13

part one: **AGGRESSION, FRUSTRATION AND THE BUSINESS CYCLE**   21

II. Suicide, Status and the Business Cycle   23

     INTRODUCTION   23

     THE GROSS RELATION BETWEEN SUICIDE AND
        THE BUSINESS CYCLE   25

     SUICIDE BY SEX   27

     SUICIDE BY RACE   33.

     SUICIDE BY AGE   36

     SUICIDE BY INCOME   38

     SUMMARY   41

III. Homicide, Status and the Business Cycle   45

     INTRODUCTION   45

     MURDER, AGGRAVATED ASSAULT AND
        THE BUSINESS CYCLE   46

     HOMICIDE BY RACE   49

     LYNCHING   51

HOMICIDE BY SEX   51
SUMMARY   52

IV. Aggression, Frustration and the Business Cycle   54
INTRODUCTION   54
INTERPRETATION   55

part two: **SOME SOCIOLOGICAL DETERMINANTS OF THE
CHOICE BETWEEN SUICIDE AND HOMICIDE**   67

V. Suicide and Social Control   69

VI. Homicide and Social Control   82
INTRODUCTION   82
DATA   82
INTERPRETATION   94

part three: **SOME PSYCHOLOGICAL DETERMINANTS OF THE
CHOICE BETWEEN SUICIDE AND HOMICIDE**   99

VII. Bases for the Legitimization of Other-oriented Aggression   101
SOCIOLOGICAL BASES   101
PSYCHOLOGICAL BASES FOR THE
LEGITIMIZATION OF OTHER-ORIENTED
AGGRESSION   103
PARENT-CHILD CORRELATES OF TWO
PSYCHOLOGICAL BASES OF LEGITIMIZATION
OF OTHER-ORIENTED AGGRESSION   106
IMPLICATIONS FOR SUICIDE AND HOMICIDE   115

VIII. Some Research Suggestions   120

APPENDICES   129

I. Previous Research   131
SUICIDE: CONTRIBUTIONS TO THEORY   131

CONTRIBUTIONS OF FACT   134

CRIME: CONTRIBUTIONS TO THEORY   138

CONTRIBUTIONS OF FACT   139

II. Correlation of Time Series—Trends and Cycles   141

THE BUSINESS CYCLE   141

THE CONCEPTS OF TRENDS AND CYCLES   142

TRENDS IN SOCIAL PHENOMENA   143

LARGE AND SMALL CYCLES   144

III. Methods: The Burns-Mitchell Technique   155

INTRODUCTION   155

SPECIFIC CYCLES   157

REFERENCE CYCLES   159

SUMMARY   162

IV. The Reaction of Cycles of Suicide to Cycles of Business   163

CORRESPONDENCE BETWEEN CYCLES OF
SUICIDE AND CYCLES OF BUSINESS   163

DIFFERENTIAL SENSITIVITY OF SUICIDE
SERIES TO PERIODS OF BUSINESS
CONTRACTION AND BUSINESS EXPANSION   167

V. Offenses Against Property and the Business Cycle   174

BURGLARY   174

ROBBERY   177

SUMMARY   179

Notes

CHAPTER I   183

CHAPTER II   183

CHAPTER III   185

CHAPTER IV   187

CHAPTER V   188

Contents

CHAPTER VI   189

CHAPTER VII   191

CHAPTER VIII   193

APPENDIX I   193

APPENDIX II   195

APPENDIX III   196

APPENDIX IV   196

APPENDIX V   196

Bibliography   199

Index   207

PREFACE

This book attempts to bring within a common framework knowledge and theories about the direction of expression of aggression which have developed independently within the disciplines of sociology, psychology and economics. The argument presented is tentative and subject to confirmation or modification by empirical test of the numerous hypotheses generated in the course of its development.

The authors gratefully acknowledge the help, criticism and encouragement given by each of the following persons: William F. Ogburn and Ernest W. Burgess of the University of Chicago; Albert J. Reiss, Jr., Vanderbilt University; Talcott Parsons and Theodore M. Mills of Harvard University; Duncan MacRae, Jr., University of California.

Special thanks are due the Laboratory of Social Relations, Harvard University, the Research Committee of the State College of Washington and the Office of the Associate Dean of Social Sciences, State College of Washington for grants aiding in the completion of the project.

Andrew F. Henry
James F. Short, Jr.

Harvard University
The State College of Washington
January, 1954.

chapter I

INTRODUCTORY STATEMENT

In 1950 about seventeen thousand persons in the United States decided life was no longer worth the struggle and died by their own hands. Another eight thousand were murdered. Roughly one out of every sixty deaths was the result either of suicide or homicide.

All of the social sciences have been concerned with the study of these acts of violence. Anthropologists have described suicide and murder in primitive societies. Experimental psychology has been concerned with aggressive behavior as a reaction to frustration and as a function of punishment. Psychoanalytic theory sees both suicide and homicide as extreme forms of aggression, the one directed against the self, the other directed against another person. Suicide is seen as a function of an excessively strict and punishing "superego" or internalized restraining mechanism of the personality which prohibits the outward expression of aggression.

Yet it is the sociologist who has been most directly concerned with these forms of violence because of their strong and persistent relationships with other sociological variables. It is the purpose of this volume to re-examine these relationships in the light of additional data presented in the following chapters and to suggest tentatively certain points of congruence between the disparate theoretical formulations which have developed independently in the various disciplines.

Suicide and homicide are treated throughout as our main dependent variables and are defined operationally in terms of the definitions governing official compilations of suicide and crime statistics.

13

Data presented in this study are limited to those available for the United States. Consequently, the study is without "cross cultural" reference in the usual sense. This decision rests upon our conviction that the probability of error of interpretation in the task which we have set would increase many fold if we jumped from culture to culture, pulling relationships out of their cultural context in haphazard fashion.

As an example, it would be desirable to test the well-known formulation of Durkheim that the reported association of religious practice with suicide was a function of the degree of cohesion of the religious group.[1] Clearly, before this could be done, the effect of status position would have to be controlled since in the United States religious practice is associated with status position. If members of a certain religious category were primarily high status members of the society, we would be unable to say whether their high suicide rate was related to their religion or to their status or to both. This problem becomes much more complex when we deal with more than one culture, since we then must understand the pattern of inter-relationship of the relevant variables in each of the cultures.

It is our hope that the propositions suggested by this study in the American culture will be tested in other cultures. This type of replicative study will help define the limits of generality of our "case study" conclusions.

Part I examines the relation of suicide and homicide to the business cycle in the United States in the search for a theoretical connection between the economic correlates of suicide and homicide and their social and psychological aspects. Three assumptions are made: (1) aggression is often a consequence of frustration; (2) business cycles produce variation in the hierarchical ranking of persons and groups; (3) frustrations are generated by interference with the "goal response" of maintaining a constant or rising position in a status hierarchy relative to the status position of others in the same status reference system.

With these assumptions, data are introduced to examine the reasonableness of the hypothesis that the reactions of both suicide and homicide to the business cycle can be consistently interpreted as aggressive reactions to frustration generated by the flow of economic forces. Certain of the earlier explanations of correlations of suicide and homicide with the business cycle are questioned. It is found that the association between homicide and alcoholism cannot account for the relation of homicide with the business cycle. Nor can Durkheim's formulation[2] based on variation in the control of social norms over behavior account for the persistent negative correlations between suicide and the business cycle.

Our data show that while suicide rises in depression and falls in prosperity, crimes of violence against persons rise in prosperity and fall during depression. Although suicide of all categories increases during depression, the degree of increase is greatest among the high status categories. The fact that the increase is greatest for the high status categories suggests that high status categories suffer a greater relative loss of status during business contraction than do low status categories. Homicide of the high status white category increases during business contraction while homicide of the low status Negro category decreases. Thus, the homicide data also suggest that high status categories suffer a greater relative loss of status during business contraction than do low status categories. As we move down the status scale, the response of suicide to business depression decreases and the response of homicide to business prosperity increases.

Since the patterns of response both of suicide and homicide to the business cycle are consistent with our frustration-aggression formulation when both acts are viewed as undifferentiated aggressive reactions to frustration generated by differential changes in status position accompanying business expansion and contraction, we assume tentatively that suicide and homicide are alike in the sense that they are both aggressive reactions to frustrations. This assumption is consistent with the clinical formulations of suicide and with the frustration-aggression hypothesis. As acts of aggresson, suicide and homicide cannot be differentiated with respect to the source of the frustration generating the aggression. Both respond in a consistent way to frustrations generated by economic forces.

Suicide and homicide become sharply differentiated aggressive acts when we consider the object of the aggression rather than its source. Two persons may be subject to an identical amount of frustration, yet one will react by turning the aggression upon himself while the other will react by directing the aggression outwardly against another person. The task of Part II is that of isolating the variables which determine the choice between suicide and homicide, given frustration of sufficent force.

Durkheim had suggested in his theoretical work on suicide that subordinate status operates to provide immunity against suicide because "it (poverty) is a restraint in itself."[3] Later writers had noted a correspondence between high status position and high suicide rates.

The available data confirm the hypothesis that status is associated positively with suicide in five of the six tests presented in Chapter V. The exception is the case of age where the decline in status in the later years is accompanied by an increase rather than the predicted decrease in suicide. When the relation between the incidence of homicide and status is examined, the hypothesis that status is associated negatively with homicide is tentatively confirmed. Age is again the exception to the predicted pattern. The decline in status in the later years is accompanied by a decrease rather than the expected increase in homicide.

The remaining structural correlates of suicide—marital status, urban-rural residence, and ecological distribution—are grouped conceptually under a variable which we shall call "strength of the relational system." This is defined as the degree of involvement in social or cathectic relationships with other persons. We assume that the relational system of the married is stronger, on the average, than is the relational system of the unmarried, and that the degree of involvement in social relationships with other persons is greater among residents of rural areas than among residents of urban areas. Within large cities, persons living in outlying residential districts are assumed to have stronger relational systems than the residents of the centrally located and more disorganized sectors of cities which are characterized by extremes of residential mobility and anonymity.

With these assumptions, the data support the hypothesis that suicide varies inversely with the strength of the relational system. The somewhat inadequate data available for homicide in general support the hypothesis that homicide varies positively with strength of the relational system.

Two propositions emerge out of these relationships. The first states a positive relation between suicide and status and a negative relation between suicide and strength of the relational system. The second states a negative relation between homicide and status and a positive relation between homicide and strength of the relational system.

The writings of Durkheim, Weber,[4] Cavan,[5] and others are introduced to generate a common element in the two empirical correlates of suicide and homicide—position in the status hierarchy and strength of the relational system. Durkheim had noted that subordinate status categories were subjected to external restraint by categories more highly placed in the status hierarchy.[6] Weber and the theorists of social and personal disorganization had noted that a fundamental condition of the maintenance of a "social" relationship was the requirement for conformity to the demands and expectations of the other person.[7]

A person of low status is required to conform to the demands and expectations of persons of higher status merely by virtue of his low status. A person involved in intense "social" interaction with another person is required to conform to the demands and expectations imposed as a condition of the relationship.

These observations may be summarized in the following proposition: the strength of external restraint to which behavior is subjected varies positively with the strength of the relational system and inversely with position in the status hierarchy. "Strength of external restraint" is defined as the degree to which behavior is required to conform to the demands and expectations of other persons.

Our empirical propositions relating suicide and homicide to status and strength of the relational system may now be restated in terms of the strength of external restraint as follows: suicide varies negatively and homicide positively with the strength of external restraint over behavior.

This formulation suggests that when external restraints are weak, aggression generated by frustration will be directed against the self and when external restraints are strong, aggression generated by frustration will be directed outwardly against another person. Two testable subsidiary hypotheses are suggested in the course of development of the argument. The first suggests a negative relation between strength of the relational system and age. If research should deny the hypothesis that the degree of involvement in social relationships decreases with increasing age, the empirical basis of our formulation would be seriously weakened. The second hypothesis predicts that the incidence of homicide will be higher in the married category than in the unmarried category. Rejection of this hypothesis would also cast doubt upon the formulation.

Two assumptions introduce the discussion of the legitimization of "other-oriented" aggression in Part III. With the assumptions— (1) that the basic and primary target of aggression is another person rather than the self and (2) that the degree to which aggression is directed outwardly against others varies positively with the degree to which other-oriented aggression is defined as legitimate by the aggressor—then "self-oriented" aggression becomes a residual category, or aggression for which outward expression is denied legitimacy.

By placing homicide at one extreme of a continuum of legitimacy of other-oriented aggression and by placing suicide at the other extreme, we are able to restate our proposition relating suicide and homicide to the strength of external restraint over behavior as follows: the degree of legitimization of other-oriented aggression consequent to aggression varies positively with the strength of external restraint over behavior. When behavior is required to conform rigidly to the demands and expectations of others (when external restraints are strong), the expression of aggression against others is legitimized. When external restraints are weak, other-oriented aggression consequent to frustration fails to be legitimized and the aggression is directed against the self.

When behavior is subjected to strong external restraint by virtue either of subordinate status or intense involvement in social relationships with other persons, it is easy to blame others when frustration occurs. But when the external restraints are weak, the self must bear the responsibility for frustration.

Examination of two psychological bases of legitimization of other-oriented aggression—super-ego strength or guilt and cardiovascular reaction during stress—leads us to the conclusion that the "psychological" legitimization of other-oriented aggression consequent to frustration varies with the degree to which the outward expression of aggression threatens the flow of nurturance and love. This tentative formulation is derived from study of the parent-child correlates of our two psychological bases of legitimization.

The psychological basis of legitimization of other-oriented aggression is used in the interpretation of differences in incidence of suicide and homicide which cannot be accounted for in terms of the degree of external restraint over behavior.

This concludes our brief introduction to the following chapters. A review of relevant research and theory on suicide and homicide is presented in Appendix I. Tests of certain of the hypotheses generated in the course of the argument are suggested in the concluding chapter.

Let us now turn to Part I, devoted to an examination of the reasonableness of the assumption that suicide and homicide are acts of aggression consequent to frustration, undifferentiated with respect to the objective source of the frustration generating the aggression. Loss of status as a function of business contraction and expansion during the economic cycle is treated as an objective source of frustration. Part I raises the question: are the empirical relationships between suicide, homicide and the business cycle congruent with the assumption that both are acts of aggression undifferentiated with respect to one objective source of frustration?

part one

AGGRESSION, FRUSTRATION

AND THE BUSINESS CYCLE

chapter II

SUICIDE, STATUS AND THE

BUSINESS CYCLE

► INTRODUCTION

This chapter presents four tests of the hypothesis that the suicide rate of high status groups correlates more highly with the business cycle than does the suicide rate of lower status groups which are subordinate in the social system. Our data show that while the correlation between suicide and the business cycle is highly negative for both high and low status categories, it is consistently more so for the higher status categories.

Detailed analyses of several suicide series reveals that troughs of suicide cycles tend to precede in time the peaks of business cycles with which they correspond. This tendency often produces an increase in suicide during the final "pre-peak" phase of business prosperity. Data fail to confirm Durkheim's explanation of this pattern in terms of the weakening of social controls over behavior during periods of "abrupt growth in power and wealth" since the pattern is stronger for females than for males, and since years with the sharpest rates of increase in the business index are invariably years of decline in suicide.

Since correlational measures as used in this chapter index the relative degree of variation in suicide, it seems reasonable to interpret

23

differences in the degree of variation or correlation in terms of differential degrees of frustration which business cycles impose on differing status categories. Our empirical finding would then suggest that high status categories suffer greater frustration during downswings of business and less frustration during upswings of business than the subordinate status categories with which they are compared.

In order to test this hypothesis, we have compared the reaction to the business cycle of suicide of males and females, of whites and Negroes, of the young and the old, and of high and low income groups. Parsons has outlined six criteria which may be used in the hierarchical ranking of broad status categories.[1] Four of his criteria, those of achievement, possession, authority and power are relevant in ranking our categories of sex, race, age and income.

The criterion of achievement, "the valued results of the actions of individuals,"[2] would place males higher than females, would rank the producing young and middle-aged higher than those beyond the retirement age of 65, and would give a higher place to those with a large income than to those with a small income. This criterion is less appropriate for the ranking of status distinctions between whites and Negroes than certain of the other criteria.

The criterion of possessions, "things, not necessarily material objects, belonging to an individual which are distinguished by the criterion of transferability,"[3] would rank the white category higher than the Negro category and would give the high income groups a loftier position than the low income groups.

Authority, "an institutionalized right to influence the actions of others" and power, a residual category defined as "non-institutionalized ability to influence others or to achieve or secure possessions"[4] are highly relevant for our ranking problem. The greater power and authority vested in whites as compared with Negroes is clear. The occupational demands on males gives them an institutionalized right to influence the actions of others which is denied, in large measure, to females. The decline in the authority of the aged has been well documented, particularly where the institution of retirement denies an occupational role to those past the age of 65. While the ability of the higher income groups to influence the actions of the lower income groups is not institutionalized, increase in influence and possessions associated with increasing income gives many prerogatives to the wealthy which are denied the poor.

In general, then, these criteria rank males above females, whites above Negroes, the young and middle-aged above the aged, and the higher income groups above the lower income groups.

Our data are presented in the sections which follow.

▶ THE GROSS RELATION BETWEEN SUICIDE
   AND THE BUSINESS CYCLE

Data.—Before examining the relation of suicide and the business cycle for varying status categories, it is important to point out that all of our suicide series correlate negatively with business fluctuations. Suicide tends to rise during periods of depression and to fall during periods of prosperity. But the negative reaction of suicide to depression is stronger than the negative reaction of suicide to prosperity.

Data presented in Appendix IV show that suicide increased during 82 per cent of the years in which Ayres' Index of Industrial Activity in the United States was falling.[5, 6] The number of suicides decreased during only 58 per cent of the years in which the index was rising.[7]

Comparison of the correspondence of peaks of suicide cycles with troughs of business cycles shows that suicide tends to reach its peak in the same year in which the business cycle reaches its trough.[8] But in over half the cases (54 per cent) suicide cycles reach their troughs a year or two before business cycles reach their peaks.[9]

These two findings, based on analysis of 23 differing suicide series, suggest that periods of business expansion prior to the business peak are accompanied by increases in the number of suicides. During the final pre-peak phase of business prosperity suicide, in about half the cases, is rising along with the business index. Suicide tends to reach its low point in over half the cases before the business cycle reaches its high point, thus accounting for the 58 per cent of the cases of concomittant rise of suicide with the business index during the final phases of business expansion.

Certain additional data presented in Appendix IV confirm this

finding. Average annual rates of rise in suicide during business contractions are about four times as great as average annual rates of
fall in suicide during business expansions.[10] Rates of increase in suicide are somewhat greater during the first half of business contraction
(the half immediately following the business peak) than during the
final or pre-trough half of the business contraction. Rates of decrease
in suicide are greater during the first half of business expansion immediately after the business trough than during the second half of
business expansion—the half immediately preceding the business
peak.[11] The suicide rate is often found to be rising along with the
business index during the final pre-peak half of business expansion.

During the initial phase of recovery in business following the
depth of the depression, suicide rates tend to decrease. As the business recovery gets under way, however, and as prosperity nears its
peak, suicide responds by ending its decline and beginning to rise.
This type of reaction accounts for the positive relation found for
many series between the suicide rate and business expansion.

While there is a marked tendency for suicide to increase during
periods of business expansion, the increase in suicide occurs most
frequently during years when the rise in the business index is very
slight. Figure 1 shows that years in which the business index showed
the sharpest rise were years in which the majority of the suicide
series reacted negatively, i.e., the rates of suicide decline.

For the 5 years in which 17 or more of the 23 suicide series showed
a rise along with the business index, the index rose an average of
8.6 per cent over the previous year. For the 4 years in which between
7 and 11 of the suicide series showed a rise, the index rose an average
of 14.5 per cent over the previous year. And for the 5 years when
all but four or five of the 23 suicide series showed a decline, the
business index rose an average of 22.2 per cent.

From these data, it is clear that sharp rates of rise in the business
index are reflected in declines in the suicide rate. The suicide rate
seems to rise with the business index only in those years immediately
preceding the business peak, not during years of rapid expansion
of business.

Discussion.—There are passages in Durkheim suggesting that
suicide should rise along with the business index during final specu-

lative phases of business cycles preceding business peaks. For example:

> It is the same if the source of the crisis is an abrupt growth of power and wealth. . . . With increased prosperity, desires increase. At the very moment when traditional rules have lost their authority, the richer prize offered these appetites stimulates them and makes them more exigent and impatient of control. . . .[12]

The data of this section give considerable support to his hypothesis. The strong tendencies for troughs of suicide cycles to precede peaks of business cycles, and for suicide to rise along with the business index during the final half of business expansion are consistent with Durkheim's hypothesis if we assume that the "crisis" comes just prior to the peak of business. But our finding that suicide increased only during those years when the rise in the business index was very slight and not during those years of "abrupt growth of power and wealth" weakens the hypothesis. We will delay interpretation of our "lead" data until we have examined differences in the behavior of suicide of males and females at the turning point of the business cycle. Let us turn now to a test of the major hypothesis of this chapter, that suicide of high status categories will be more highly correlated with the business cycle than suicide of lower status categories.

▶ SUICIDE BY SEX

Introduction.—Our hypothesis predicts that suicide of males will correlate more highly with the business cycles than suicide of females. The relative status of males and females is connected with the economic services they perform. While increase in technology and the growth of culture has created many new economic opportunities for women, these opportunities lag behind those made available to men. Many occupations are still closed to women. Opportunities for upward mobility are severely restricted and are often contingent upon the mobility of the husband. Feminine roles, in many cases, lie "outside" the dominant "achievement-oriented" American value system.[13] If business cycles affect the suicide rate of groups with high status more than the suicide rate of subordinate groups with lower status, we would expect suicide of males to correlate more highly with business conditions than would suicide of females.

Data.—The comparisons of Table 1 indicate that business cycles

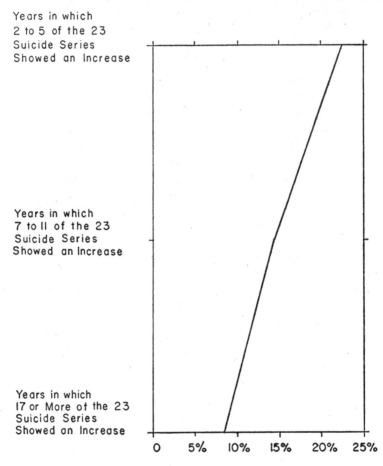

Years in which
2 to 5 of the 23
Suicide Series
Showed an Increase

Years in which
7 to 11 of the 23
Suicide Series
Showed an Increase

Years in which
17 or More of the 23
Suicide Series
Showed an Increase

0   5%   10%   15%   20%   25%

Average Percent Increase in Ayres'
Index of Business Activity Over
Previous Year

Figure 1. Positive Correspondence of Suicide to Business Expansions,
and Per Cent Increase in the Business Index.

are more highly correlated with suicide of males than with suicide of females. The column headed "Suicide Category" in Table 1 lists different breakdowns of the American population for which data on suicide by sex are available. For seven of the nine cases, suicide of males correlates more highly with business cycles than suicide of females. Throughout the correlational analysis, the test of replication is applied rather than the test of the standard error of individual time series correlation coefficients.[14]

Table 1—Correlation between Business Cycles and Suicide[a]

Suicide Category	Males	Females
U.S.D.R.S.[b]	−.76	−.71
U.S.D.R.S.—White	−.86	−.82
U.S.D.R.S.—Non-white	−.71	−.82
U.S.D.R.S.—Age 15-24	−.83	−.69
U.S.D.R.S.—Age 25-34	−.88	−.71
U.S.D.R.S.—Age 35-44	−.74	−.75
U.S.D.R.S.—Age 45-54	−.79	−.67
U.S.D.R.S.—Age 55-64	−.79	−.78
U.S.D.R.S.—Age 65-74	−.49	−.20

Suicide Category	White	Non-White
U.S.D.R.S.	−.81	−.38
U.S.D.R.S.—Male	−.86	−.71
U.S.D.R.S.—Female	−.82	−.82
U.S.D.R.S.—Urban	−.57	−.47
U.S.D.R.S.—Rural	−.73	−.50

a. Equations of trend lines are presented in Appendix II, Table 2. Each series is numbered. The series of suicide of males in the United States Death Registration States is listed as No. 1. Coefficients in the above table are here presented with their corresponding reference numbers in parentheses.
Males: −.76 (1); −.86 (3); −.71 (5); −.83 (7); −.88 (9); −.74 (11); −.79 (13); −.79 (15); −.49 (17).
Females: −.71 (2); −.82 (4); −.82 (6); −.69 (8); −.71 (10); −.75 (12); −.67 (14); −.78 (16); −.20 (18).
White: −.81 (19); −.86 (3); −.82 (4); −.57 (21); −.73 (23).
Non-White: −.38 (20); −.71 (5); −.82 (6); −.47 (22); −.50 (24).
b. United States Death Registration States are those states for which data on suicide are collected by the United States Bureau of Vital Statistics.

The suicide rate of males in the United States from 1900-1947 is correlated −.76 with fluctuations in business.[15] The relation between the suicide rate of females and business cycles is slightly lower. The difference between the coefficients is so small, however, that further cases are needed to show that the relationship is sustained.

Examination of the relationship between business fluctuations and suicide of males and females holding race constant provides further tests of the hypothesis. Dublin and Bunzel found that the suicide rate of white males was more sensitive to their business index than suicide of white females.[16] Our data confirm this finding. Unexpected differences between the sexes appear when business cycles are correlated with suicide cycles of the non-whites. Suicide of non-white females is more highly correlated with business fluctuations than suicide of non-white males. Suicide of the non-white woman is as sensitive to business cycles as suicide of the white woman, while the non-white male is markedly less sensitive than the white male.

A number of additional comparisons of sensitivity of suicide of males and females to business cycles are possible when suicides are broken into age groups. For four of the six age groups, including ages 15-24, 25-34, 45-54, and 65-74, suicide of males is markedly more sensitive to business cycles than suicide of females of the same age. In the other two age groupings, the coefficients of correlation are approximately equal.

In our section on the gross relation between suicide and the business cycle, we introduced data showing that suicide tends to reach its trough before the business cycle reaches its peak. The tendency for troughs of suicide to precede peaks of business and for peaks of suicide to precede troughs of business are presented separately for series of suicide of males and females in Table 2.

Table 2—Correspondence of Turning Points of Suicide and Business Cycles, by Sex*

Series of Suicide by Sex	AT BUSINESS PEAKS		AT BUSINESS TROUGHS	
	Per Cent of Suicide Troughs Occurring a Year or Two Earlier	Per Cent of Suicide Troughs Occurring the Same Year	Per Cent of Suicide Peaks Occurring a Year or Two Earlier	Per Cent of Suicide Peaks Occurring the Same Year
Males (10 series)	.53	.47	.08	.92
Females (9 series)	.70	.30	.59	.41

* Data from Tables 1 and 2, Appendix IV. Cases where the suicide turning points follow the business cycle turning points in time and cases of non-correspondence are excluded.

Suicide of females reaches its trough and starts to rise before the business cycle reaches its peak with somewhat greater frequency than suicide of males but the tendency is pronounced for both sex categories. Suicide of females is found to reach its peak and starts to fall before the business cycle reaches its trough in over half the cases, while suicide of males consistently reaches its peak in the same year that the business cycle reaches its lowest point.

The fact that cycles of male suicide are more closely related to business cycles than are cycles of female suicide is further illustrated in Table 3. The response of male suicide both to expansions and contractions in business is more strongly negative than the response of suicide of females. But again for the males, there is a marked tendency for suicide to rise along with the business cycle. These two tables are congruent with the correlational result that suicide of males is more sensitive to the fluctuations of economic conditions than is suicide of females. They show, further, that both troughs and peaks of female suicide "lead" the corresponding turning points of business, thus accounting at least in part for the lower correlations between female suicide and the business cycle.

Table 3—Behavior of Suicide Series During Years In Which the Business Index Was Rising and During Years In Which the Business Index Was Falling, by Sex[a]

	YEARS IN WHICH BUSINESS INDEX WAS RISING		YEARS IN WHICH BUSINESS INDEX WAS FALLING	
Series of Suicide by Sex	Per Cent of Years in Which Suicide Was Falling	Per Cent of Years in Which Suicide Was Rising	Per Cent of Years in Which Suicide Was Rising	Per Cent of Years in Which Suicide Was Falling
Males (10 series)	.64[b]	.36[b]	.96[d]	.04[d]
Females (9 series)	.48[c]	.52[c]	.60[e]	.40[e]

a. Data from Tables 7 and 8, Appendix IV. The few cases where suicide remained constant during changes in the business index are excluded.
b. Percentages based on 149 cases.
c. Percentages based on 128 cases.
d. Percentages based on 72 cases.
e. Percentages based on 63 cases.

Tables 4 and 5 demonstrate the same relationship in a slightly different way. Suicide of males (Table 4) falls faster during prosperity and rises faster during depression than suicide of females.

Table 5 illustrates the tendency for suicide of both males and females to rise during the second half of business expansion, and that this tendency is stronger for females than for males.

The rate of fall of male suicide following the business trough exceeds the rate of fall of female suicide during the same period. The rate of rise of male suicide immediately following the business peak exceeds the rate of rise of female suicide. For both sex categories,

Table 4—Average Annual Rate of Change in Suicide of Males and Females during Phases of the Business Cycle*

Suicide Series	Average Rate of Fall in Suicide During Expansion Phases of the Business Cycle	Average Rate of Rise in Suicide During Contraction Phases of the Business Cycle
Males, U.S.D.R.S., 1900-1941	−2.3	+9.5
Females, U.S.D.R.S., 1900-1941	−0.5	+2.9

* See Appendix IV for methods of computation of rates of change.

suicide increases more rapidly during the early part of business contraction than during the final half of business contraction but the difference is more marked for males than for females.

Discussion.—Of the nine cases of correlational comparison, all but three conform to the predicted pattern. Two of the non-conforming cases yield approximately the same coefficient for both males and females. The single important exception to the expected pattern is the case of the non-whites. In the United States, the bulk of this category is made up of the Negro population. Suicide of non-white females correlates more highly with the business cycle than suicide of non-white males, thus violating the predicted pattern.

Table 5—Average Annual Rate of Change of Suicide of Males and Females during Phases of Expansion and Contraction in the Business Cycle[a]

	AVERAGE ANNUAL RATE OF CHANGE			
	DURING PHASES OF BUSINESS EXPANSION		DURING PHASES OF BUSINESS CONTRACTION	
Suicide Series	First Half	Second Half	First Half	Second Half
Males[b]	−3.5	+0.3	+10.6	+0.1
Females[c]	−1.0	+1.8	+ 3.5	+2.4

a. See Appendix IV for methods of computation.
b. Series of male suicide, U.S.D.R.S., 1900-1940.
c. Series of female suicide, U.S.D.R.S., 1900-1940.

The instability inherent in the technique of time series correlation forces us to exercise care in the interpretation of findings based on a single case. Yet it is worthy of notice that the exception to the general pattern involves the status relationship between Negro males and Negro females.

The role of the female in the Negro family, as compared with the male, may explain the greater sensitivity of her suicide rate to the business cycles. Historical circumstances have forced her to assume a large share of responsibility for the economic support of her family. Her position of high status within the Negro community may well act to increase her probability of suicide as a function of the business cycle.[17] The relatively high correlation between suicide of Negro females and the business cycle may also be related to the effect of business conditions on the rate of desertion among non-whites.

When our analysis of correspondence of turning points of suicide cycles and turning points of business cycles was presented, holding sex constant, we found that suicide of females "leads" the business cycle at both the business peak and the business trough. There is a lesser tendency for troughs of male suicide to "lead" the business peak and no evidence that peaks of male suicide tend to precede business troughs. These findings, supported by the fact that male suicide increases during depression and decreases during prosperity with greater frequency than female suicide, confirm our correlational results. Additional confirmation is provided by the differential rates of change of male and female suicide during business expansion and contraction. Suicide of males reacts to business fluctuations more rapidly than does suicide of females.

In the summary section of this chapter, our data showing tendencies for suicide turning points to precede in time turning points of business cycles are presented graphically, together with some tentative interpretation. These data have been introduced here because they provide additional confirmation of our hypothesis that suicide of males, our high status category, is more sensitive to the business cycle than suicide of females, the category occupying a more subordinate status position in the American socio-economic system.

► SUICIDE BY RACE

Introduction.—Extreme differences in status mark the relationship between Negro and white persons in American society. A caste system prevents the Negro from enjoying the economic opportunities and status position available to white persons. While vertical mobility exists within the limits of his caste, it is difficult, and in most cases impossible, for the Negro to cross the caste line. The color line places a hard limit on ambitions whetted in times of business expansion. The white person in American society is not subjected to these restraints. The limits of a lower caste do not temper his aspirations.

The rigidly defined distinctions between white and Negro in American society force the Negro to live in, and adjust to, a subordinate status position. We would predict, therefore, that business fluctuations would affect suicide of white persons more strongly than suicide of non-white persons.

Data.—Data presented in Table 1 indicate that the suicide rate of white persons in the United States is more sensitive to business cycles than the suicide rate of non-white persons. In four of the five cases of racial comparisons, suicide of the white categories is found to be more highly correlated with the business cycles than suicide of the non-white categories. In the fifth case, that of white and non-white females, the coefficients are equal.

The suicide rate of white persons in the United States from 1910-1947 is correlated —.81 with business cycles while the suicide rate of non-whites is markedly less sensitive, with a coefficient of —.38. This sharp difference in the effect of economic factors is reduced when coefficients are computed for the period 1923-1947. The coefficient for whites rises slightly to —.86[18] while the coefficient for non-whites nearly doubles in size becoming —.74.[19] Fluctuations in business are reflected more markedly in the suicide rate of whites in both time periods.

Suicide of white males in the United States from 1923-1947 is also more sensitive to fluctuations in economic conditions than is suicide of non-white males. But coefficients between business cycles and suicide of white and non-white females are equal.

In urban areas,[20] business cycles from 1910-1947 correlate more highly with suicide of whites than with suicide of non-whites. The difference in sensitivity of suicide to business cycles between whites and non-whites may be more pronounced in rural areas.[21] The coefficient for rural whites is —.73 while the coefficient for rural non-whites is —.50.

Discussion.—Analysis of four of the five categories of suicide broken down by race indicates that suicide of whites is more sensitive to business cycles than is suicide of non-whites. No difference appears in the comparison of the correlations for white and non-white females. These findings lend additional confirmation to our hypothesis that suicide of those groups most subordinated in the social system will be the least sensitive to fluctuations in business conditions. This conclusion stands up when we compare the sensitivity of whites with that of non-whites as well as when we compare the sensitivity of males and females.[22]

The higher sensitivity of suicides of non-whites to economic conditions since 1923 may be explained by a combination of factors. The period following World War I was one of great influx of Negroes from rural areas of the South into urban centers of the North. Part of the explanation may lie in this migration. The period since 1923 has seen increasing economic and social opportunities opened to the Negro. The improved economic status associated with migration has removed from the Negro many restraints formerly operating upon him, and the development of protective and equalitarian legislation has served to lessen the status differential between races.

If this interpretation of the marked increase in sensitivity of non-white suicide to business cycles since 1923 is correct, it gives additional strength to our hypothesis. With the migration northward, and the consequent improvement of the subordinate position enforced upon the Negro in the rural south, we would expect the non-white suicide rate to reflect increasingly the fluctuations in economic conditions.

Suicide of white females and non-white females is equally sensitive to business cycles. Status differentials between the sexes differ within the Negro and white groups. Historical factors in the development of the Negro family have given the female a position of economic responsibility. A higher proportion of Negro families have females as heads of the family than do white families. Rates of desertion and illegitimacy are higher, leaving females burdened with the economic support of the family.

Lower caste status of the Negro woman, as compared with the white woman, may be roughly compensated by her high status when compared with that of the Negro male. On the one hand, her caste position in relation to society as a whole may act to protect her from suicide during depressions. On the other hand, her high status within her own caste group may operate to increase her susceptibility.

Our data support the conclusion that suicide of non-white persons in the United States is less sensitive to fluctuations in economic conditions than is suicide of the white population. The data support our hypothesis that suicide of those groups most subordinated in the social system is less affected by business fluctuations than suicide of those groups enjoying higher status positions.

▶   SUICIDE BY AGE

Introduction.—Age has proven to be an important variable in analyses of structural relationships within American society. Parsons has discussed the relationship of age grading to the kinship structure, formal education, occupation, and community participation.[23]

Breakdowns by age provide some control over related factors such as occupation. Economic activity varies with age and rates of labor force participation for persons over 65 are lower than rates for those between 15 and 65.

Parsons characterizes the adult male role as one involving prestige and responsibility.

It is of fundamental significance to the sex role structure of the adult age levels that the normal man has a "job" which is fundamental to his social status in general. It is perhaps not too much to say that only in very exceptional cases can an adult man be genuinely self-respecting and enjoy a respected status in the eyes of others if he does not "earn a living" in an approved occupational role. Not only is this a matter of his own economic support but, generally speaking, his occupational status is the primary source of the income and class status of his wife and children.[24]

The sharp decline in status, associated with the institution of retirement at the age of 65, has been documented by numerous studies.[25] While it is difficult to distinguish age groupings between 15 and 65 in terms of relative status, there is little question about the loss of prestige and status after age 65, as compared with younger groups. Persons over 65 suffer a decline in occupational participation and a subsequent decline in status. We would predict that this age grouping would run less risk of suicide associated with business cycles than any of the other age groups from 15-65.

Data.—Suicide rates by sex for ten-year age groupings were correlated with the business cycles in the United States from 1920-

1947. While the coefficients for males in the five age groups from 15-65 range from —.74 to —.88 (Table 1), the coefficient for males in the age group 65-74 is —.49. Examination of the data for females by age yields a similar confirmation of the hypothesis. While the coefficients for females in the five age groups from 15 to 64 range from —.67 to —.78, the coefficient for females in the age group 65 to 74 is —.20.

Striking declines in sensitivity occur for both males and females upon reaching age 65. There is little doubt that the correlation between suicide and the business cycle is much lower for both males and females between ages 65 to 74 than for any other age category.

Discussion.—Sensitivity of suicide of males and females to business cycles declines after age 65. This finding is congruent with our hypothesis since the decline in status associated with old age in a highly developed technological society has been noted in numerous studies. Persons, particularly males, of this age group relinquish their jobs. Unlike old age in primitive society, the person past 65 is no longer looked to for advice and counsel.

A word of caution is in order here. The finding with respect to age is based on only two cases, the categories of male and female in the United States. Other cases are needed before this conclusion can be placed on more than a tentative basis. In addition, data by age are necessarily confounded by the effect of marital status. Single persons are found primarily among the young and widowed persons are found primarily among the aged so it is conceivable that our finding is only spuriously related to age and is in reality a function of the effect of marital status. Data for suicide, holding both age and marital status constant, are not available through time.

A time series of suicide by marital status was available for Cook County, Illinois, running from 1905 to 1947. Suicide of the married correlates —.77[26] with business cycles while suicide of single persons correlates —.50.[27]

Three studies of the sociological impact of the depression on the family,[28, 29, 30] support the thesis of a disturbance in the authority and role structure of the family. The loss of authority of the unemployed husband cited by Komarovsky would lead to the suggestion that the relatively greater sensitivity of suicide of the married as compared with the single might become more pronounced if suicide data were available for males by marital status. Further, if data by age are confounded by the effect of marital status, then certainly data by marital status are confounded by the effect of age. But the only available series of suicide by marital status indicates that the married are more sensitive to business cycles than the single. While the old are less sensitive than the young, single persons, who on the average are younger, are less sensitive than the married. It is probable that suicide by both age and marital status are correlated independently with business cycles, but the absence of time series suicide data, with age, marital status and sex held constant, makes it impossible to isolate each factor.[31]

The findings by age, however, certainly do not contradict the hypothesis and are in the direction predicted. The lowered status position of the aged in American society is reflected in the lower degree of sensitivity of their suicide rate to business cycles, as compared with the younger age groups.

▶   SUICIDE BY INCOME

Introduction.—We have predicted that the suicide rate of the higher income groups would be more sensitive to fluctuations in business than suicide of the lower income groups. If those groups most subordinated in the society are best protected from suicide fluctuating with the business cycle, the low status associated with low income should make for relatively low correlations between suicide of marginal income groups and the business cycle as compared with groups in the higher income brackets.

Data.—Time series of suicide by income are not available for the United States. In order to get some control over this variable, we have compiled the ecological distribution of suicide in Chicago, based on rates for community areas during the depression years 1930-1932 and the prosperity years of 1939-1941. While the years 1939-1941 were not peak years of business, they do represent a period of relative prosperity uncomplicated by war. The year 1932 was a year in which the business cycle reached its trough. The average Ayres' Index of Industrial Production[32] during 1930-1932 was 28 per cent below the long-term trend of business while the comparable average during 1939-1941 was 5.5 per cent above the trend. The suicide rate per 100,000 residents of Chicago dropped about 27 per cent between 1930-1932 and 1939-1941.

One of the statistical indices which has proved useful in the measurement of income is median rental. Data on median monthly rental are available for the 75 community areas in Chicago for the decennial census years of 1930 and 1940.[33] We have rank-ordered community areas by median rental and selected the 16 areas with the highest rentals in both 1930 and 1940,[34] and the 16 areas with the lowest rentals in both 1930 and 1940.[35]

The suicide rate dropped in both the high rent and low rent areas between 1930-1932 and 1939-1941. But the per cent decrease was greater in the high rent areas than in the low rent areas. The rate declined 27.1 per cent in the high rent areas but dropped only 17.7 per cent in the low rent areas.

While this finding is in the direction predicted, it may merely reflect the fact that Negroes, who tend to be concentrated in the low rent areas, are less sensitive to the effects of the business cycle than are white persons. So we have removed those community areas with non-white populations from our group of high rent and low rent areas and re-computed the percentage declines in the suicide rate from the 1929-1932 depression period as compared to the 1939-1941 prosperity period.

The differential sensitivity to suicide of high and low rent areas is now more striking than before. The per cent decline in the high rent areas between 1930-1932 and 1939-1941 is over four times as great as the per cent decline in the low rent areas. The suicide rate in 14 high rent community areas with 100 per cent white populations dropped 28.9 per cent between 1930-1932 and 1939-1941 while the rate in 13 low rent community areas containing 100 per cent white populations dropped only 6.1 per cent.[36]

Our conclusion that suicide of the higher income groups is affected by the business cycle more than suicide of the lower income groups is subject to several limitations. The available data make it possible to compare suicide rates at a trough and relative peak period of only one business cycle. The business cycle was undergoing expansion during the period from 1930-1932 to 1939-1941. Our data do not cover the case of business contraction.

Further, the comparisons made here with respect to median rental, or income, rest on the assumption that percentage drops in suicide rates between the two periods reflect the cyclical expansion in business during the decade, and are not a function of a declining secular trend in suicide.

Finally, this conclusion rests on the assumption of the validity of ecological correlations when the only comparison being made is a comparison between two different periods in time.[37]

Discussion.—Subject to the limitations set forth in the preceding paragraphs, our data indicate that the suicide rate of the economically privileged is more sensitive to fluctuations of business than is that of the poor. While there is a sharp difference in the suicide rate of high rental groups during the 1930-1932 trough years of business and the 1939-1941 relative peak years of business, the suicide rate of the low rental groups in Chicago remains relatively constant. This is true in spite of the fact that the absolute rates are higher in the low income areas during both periods, when community areas with non-white populations are removed from the analysis.

We have related the concept of "egoistic" suicide to the empirical studies showing high rates of suicide in the central sectors of cities with high rates of residential mobility and social disorganization. The concept of "anomie" was considered applicable to the type of suicide correlating with business cycles, and conceived to be a function of vertical mobility.

The ecological distribution of suicide in Chicago does not change markedly with the business cycle. The same areas with the highest suicide rates in 1930-1932 tend to be the areas with the highest suicide rates in 1939-1941. To a lesser extent, areas with the lowest rates in the depression period are areas with the lowest rates in the prosperity period. The high rate areas are concentrated in the central, disorganized sections of the city and reflect egoistic suicide. Many of these areas are of relatively low economic status. While residents of these areas are most subject to egoistic suicide, they seem to be particularly immune to anomic suicide. The latter seems restricted to those who, freed from the bonds of subordinate status, enjoy the satisfactions of high economic position.

▶ SUMMARY

We have examined the differential sensitivity to suicide as a function of business cycles of various categories of the American population which vary in terms of the degree of social subordination to which they are subjected. In each of our four cases, the group with the higher status position reacts more violently to fluctuations of business than does the subordinate status category with which it is compared.

Suicide of males is more sensitive than suicide of females. True, the differences in correlations between the sexes are not marked, but neither is the differential in status. The "exception," the finding that the non-white female's suicide rate is more sensitive than that of the non-white male, lends strength to our hypothesis when the high prestige position of the female in the Negro family is taken into consideration.

Suicide of white persons is more sensitive than suicide of the non-white persons. Here, the status differential is sharp. The rapid rise in sensitivity of the non-white since the northward migration of the Southern Negro gives further support to the argument that a loosening of the restrictions that go with subordinate status paves the way for exposure to anomic suicide.

Suicide of persons under 65 is more sensitive to the fluctuations of economic conditions than is suicide of those suffering the subordinate status which comes with retirement in an age of rapid social change. While this finding must await suicide data holding both age and marital status constant, the high rates of sensitivity are consistent for the five age groupings from 15-65 for both sexes, and the decline for those between 65-74 is sharp.

Suicide of persons living in high rent areas in Chicago was more sensitive to the expansion in business during the decade of the thirties than suicide of persons living in low rent areas. While the suicide rate in high rent areas dropped sharply between 1930-1932 and 1939-1941, the suicide rate in low rent areas remained relatively constant.

Persons subject to the deprivations of low economic status, as indexed by low rentals, are better protected from suicide accompanying cycles of business than those who have risen to higher economic positions.

Durkheim had suggested that abrupt speculative increases in the business cycle were accompanied by increases in suicide and interpreted this phenomenon as a function of the weakening of social controls over behavior at the same time that the "passions" and desires of individuals were increasing. Our data also indicate that suicide increases during the final "pre-peak" half of business prosperity, but only during years when the increase in the business index is very slight and not during years of "abrupt" increase.

By examining the same relationships, with sex held constant, we find that the tendency for suicide to rise during the final half of business expansion is stronger for females (our lower status category) than for the higher status males. These relationships are graphed in Figure 2.

If Durkheim's explanation were correct, we would expect (1) that years of rapid rates of rise in the business index would be those years in which suicide would also increase, and (2) suicide of males, the category engaging in business and financial speculation, would be more subject to the deleterious effects of abrupt rises in business than suicide of females who for the most part do not participate in this form of financial diversion.

Both of these predictions based on Durkheim's interpretation fail to be substantiated. During years of rapid rise in the business index, suicide tends to fall. And when it does rise along with the business index during the final phases of business expansion, the increase occurs primarily among females.

Figure 3 shows the pattern of response of suicide of males and females at the business trough. While the peak of suicide among males occurs in the same year as the trough of business, the peak of female suicide occurs before the business trough is reached.

In summary, we have shown that suicide rises in depression and falls in prosperity for all of our status categories. Durkheim's prediction that suicide should rise during speculative phases of business prosperity because of the weakening of social controls over behavior and the intensity of the "passions" is not substantiated. The tendency for suicide of females to reach its maximum before the depth of the depression is reached has been interpreted in terms of the lower status of females relative to males.

Our major research hypothesis that suicide of higher status

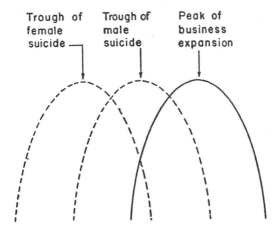

Figure 2. Behavior of Suicide of Males and Females during Business Expansion. Troughs of Male Suicide Precede Business Peaks in Time and Troughs of Female Suicide Precede Troughs of Male Suicide in Time.

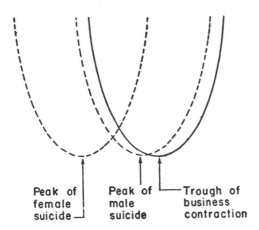

Figure 3. Behavior of Suicide of Males and Females during Business Contraction. Peaks of Male Suicide Occur in Years of Business Troughs while Peaks of Female Suicide Precede Business Troughs in Time.

categories is more sensitive to frustrations produced by the business cycle than suicide of lower status categories subordinated in the social system has been substantiated in each of four tests. Before introducing our interpretation of this result, let us examine in the following chapter the relation between homicide, status and the business cycle. In the final chapter of Part I our findings on suicide will be related conceptually to our findings on homicide and points of congruence between the two formulations will be made explicit.

chapter III

HOMICIDE, STATUS AND THE

BUSINESS CYCLE

► INTRODUCTION

Data presented in Chapter II showed that suicide of high status group-ings of the American population was more sensitive to frustrations generated by business cycles than suicide of low status groupings. While correlations between suicide and the business cycle were found to be negative for both high and low status groups, they were consistently higher for the highest status categories.

Data are introduced in this Chapter showing that homicide and aggravated assault are correlated positively with the business cycle.[1] While suicide increases during depression, homicide decreases. While suicide drops during prosperity, homicide increases. The traditional view that the positive correlation between homicide and the business cycle can be explained by the increase of alcoholism during pros-perity is shown to be incorrect in view of the fact that the relation between homicide and alcoholism vanishes when the effect of the business cycle is held constant.

Our prediction that homicide of low status categories will have a higher positive correlation with the business cycle than homicide of the higher status categories is confirmed by a reversal in the direction of the correlation between homicide and the business cycle when the effect of race is held constant.

45

► MURDER, AGGRAVATED ASSAULT AND
   THE BUSINESS CYCLE

Twenty-three time series of violent crimes against the person known
to the police were correlated with the business cycle. The coefficients are presented in Table 1. In most of the cases, trend lines
were fitted to cut off both large and small cycles.[2] Nineteen of the
23 coefficients are positive. Three of the four deviant cases are
for individual cities where instability inherent in time series correlation technique is at a maximum because of the small number of
cases. Seven of the nine murder series correlate positively and 12
of the 14 aggravated assault series correlate positively with economic conditions.

*Table 1—Correlations between Crimes of Violence Against the Person and
the Business Cycle, by Size of Cycle*

	RELATION WITH BUSINESS CYCLE	
Type of Crime	Using Large Cycles	Using Small Cycles
MURDER		
11 Cities, 1929-41/1946-49[a]	.59	.39
11 Cities, 1929-41[a]		−.07
55 Cities, 1930-41/1946-49[b]	.32	.44
55 Cities, 1930-41[b]		.20
Los Angeles, 1925-41		−.35
Baltimore, 1928-41/1946-49	.69	.51
AGGRAVATED ASSAULT		
9 Cities, 1929-41/1946-49[c]	.64	.31
9 Cities, 1929-41[c]		.43
53 Cities, 1930-41/1946-49[d]	.59	.51
53 Cities, 1930-41[d]		.53
Los Angeles, 1925-41	.60	.42
Portland, Oregon, 1925-41	−.31	.25
Rochester, 1928-41/1946-49	−.16	.11

a. Baltimore, Buffalo, Chicago, Cincinnati, Cleveland, Denver, Detroit, Kansas City (Kansas),
Los Angeles, Rochester, Wichita.
b. Akron, Albany, Birmingham, Boston, Bridgeport, Cambridge, Canton, Charlotte, Columbus
(Ohio), Dayton, Elizabeth, El Paso, Erie, Fall River, Flint, Ft. Worth, Gary, Grand Rapids, Hart-
ford, Indianapolis, Jacksonville, Knoxville, Long Beach, Miami, Milwaukee, Minneapolis, Nashville,
Newark (N. J.), New Haven, New Orleans, Norfolk, Oakland, Oklahoma City, Omaha, Peoria,
Portland (Ore.), Providence, Sacramento, St. Louis, Salt Lake City, San Antonio, San Diego, San
Francisco, Scranton, Seattle, Somerville, Spokane, Springfield (Mass.), Tacoma, Tampa, Toledo,
Utica, Washington (D.C.), Wilmington (Del.), Youngstown.
c. Includes all the cities under (a) above except Baltimore and Chicago.
d. Includes all the cities under (b) above except Knoxville, Newark, Portland, and Tacoma. In
addition, data for Lowell and Richmond are included.

Table 2—Behavior of Violent Crimes Against the Person during Years in Which the Business Index Was Falling

Phase of the Business Cycle	NUMBER OF YEARS IN WHICH INCIDENCE OF CRIME	
	Was Falling	Was Rising
Prosperity[a]	2	2
Transition[b]	11	1
Depression[c]	2	0
Total	15	3

a. Business index is above the long term trend during periods of "prosperity."
b. Movements in the business index which cross the long-term trend line.
c. Business index is below the long term trend during periods of "depression."

Table 3—Behavior of Violent Crimes Against the Person during Years In Which the Business Index Was Rising

Phase of the Business Cycle[*]	NUMBER OF YEARS IN WHICH THE INCIDENCE OF CRIME	
	Was Rising	Was Falling
Prosperity	7	5
Transition	3	5
Depression	14	10
Total	24	20

* See preceding Table for definition of phases of the business cycle.

Tables 2 and 3 report the sensitivity of murder and aggravated assault to changes in the business index during periods of prosperity, transition, and depression.[3] It is notable that there is no clear-cut positive relation between these crimes and business during business expansion. Except for periods of prosperity, however, downward movement of the economic cycle brings with it downward movement of these crimes. Too few cases are represented for generalization, but the positive relation between crimes of violence against the person and the business cycle appears from these data to be due primarily to downward movement of business during transition and depression phases of the economic cycle.

A number of writers have suggested that the positive correlation between violent crimes against persons and the business cycle could be accounted for by the positive correlation of alcoholism with the business cycle. Thomas found high positive correlations between per capita consumption of beer, and of "spirits," and the business cycle for England and Wales. She also found high positive correlations between the business cycle and both prosecutions for drunkenness and death rates from alcoholism. She found only small and insignificant positive correlations between violent crimes against persons and the business cycle.[4]

Radzinowicz observed that, in Poland, the curve of "the group of offenses against the person, and especially assault and homicide . . . follows closely that of the consumption of alcohol."[5]

The factor of alcoholism is difficult to measure in this country because of the existence of national prohibition during the early years of the study.[6] Using "deaths due to alcoholism" as an index, Linn has found a positive correlation of fluctuations of this series with the business cycle of 0.39, for the years 1919-47.[7] Linn includes the war years in his study. Including only the pre-war years, 1929-41, these variables have a positive correlation of 0.47.[8]

Aggravated assault, which correlates positively (0.43) with the business cycle for the period 1929-41 also correlates positively with deaths due to alcoholism for this same period (0.41).

Murders, with a slight tendency towards a negative relation with business for this period (—0.07), also correlate negatively with alcoholism (—0.22).

The assault data suggest that the positive correlation between assault and alcoholism could be accounted for by the positive correlation of each with the business cycle. The murder-alcohol data are more difficult to interpret.

We have shown that murders show only an unstable tendency to increase during years of prosperity and consequently must account for the overall positive correlations between murder and the business cycle by the consistent declines in murder during years of depression. In the following section, we will show that when race is held constant, the correlation between homicide and the business cycle is strongly negative for white persons and strongly positive for Negroes.

In view of this demonstration of the effect of the variable of race on the relation between murder and the business cycle, we will delay our examination of the effect of alcoholism on the correlation between murder and the business cycle until we have explored the effect of race on these relationships.

▶ HOMICIDE BY RACE

Good time series data on rates of homicide of Negroes and whites do not exist. A fairly good approximation may be had, however, with cause of death data, since Negroes tend to murder other Negroes and white persons tend to murder other white persons.[9] Six series of deaths by homicide were analyzed, three each for whites and non-whites. Table 4 presents the results of correlation analysis of these homicide series and the business cycle.

Table 4—Correlation between Business Cycles and Six Series of Deaths by Homicide, by Race*

Series	CORRELATION WITH BUSINESS INDEX	
	White	Non-white
U.S.D.R.S. of 1900, 1910-16/19-40	−.51	.49
U.S.D.R.S. of 1910, 1910-16/19-40	−.63	.38
U.S.D.R.S. of 1920, 1920-40	−.80	.26

* Trend lines fitted to these homicide series, and to the business index, are found in Appendix II, Tables 3 and 4.

In each of the three cases of comparison by race, homicide of white persons correlates negatively with the business cycle while homicide of non-white persons correlates positively with the business cycle. The Table shows further that the size of the negative correlation of white homicide with the business cycle has been increasing in recent years while the size of the positive correlation between non-white homicide and the business cycle has been decreasing.

In an earlier section, data were presented showing a relationship between alcoholism and homicide. Numerous writers have interpreted the positive relation between crimes of violence and the business cycle as a spurious function of the relation of each with the degree of alcoholism.

Data are presented in Table 5 showing positive correlations between alcoholism and homicide for non-white persons and negative correlations between alcoholism and homicide for whites. Table 6 shows that deaths by alcoholism increase during prosperity and decrease during depression among both racial categories.

Table 5—Correlations between Deaths by Homicide and Deaths by Alcoholism, by Race*

| | COEFFICIENT OF CORRELATION | |
Series	White	Non-white
U.S.D.R.S. of 1900, 1910-16/1919/1921-40	—.45	.39
U.S.D.R.S. of 1910, 1910-16/1919/1921-40	—.55	.40
U.S.D.R.S. of 1920, 1920-1940	—.70	.42

* Trend lines fitted to the homicide and alcohol series are presented in Appendix II, Table 4.

Table 6—Correlations between Business Cycles and Six Series of Deaths by Alcoholism, by Race*

| | CORRELATION WITH BUSINESS INDEX | |
Series	White	Non-white
U.S.D.R.S. of 1900, 1910-16/1919/1921-40	.75	.65
U.S.D.R.S. of 1910, 1910-16/1919/1921-40	.80	.74
U.S.D.R.S. of 1920, 1920-40	.83	.75

* Trend lines fitted to the Alcohol and Business Series are presented in Appendix II, Tables 3 and 4.

We have used the technique of partial correlation to test the hypothesis that the correlations between homicide and alcoholism will vanish when the effect of the business cycle is removed.

When the effect of the business cycle is held constant through the use of partial correlation, the coefficient of —0.45 between alcoholism and homicide of whites in the 1900 Death Registration States drops to —0.12. The coefficient of 0.39 between alcoholism and homicide of non-whites similarly drops to 0.11.[10]

The partial correlations between homicide and alcoholism in the Death Registration States of 1910 are only —0.11 for whites and 0.19 for non-whites.

These data show that the negative relation between homicide and alcoholism of whites and the positive relation between homicide and alcoholism of Negroes both "wash out" when the effect of the business cycle is held constant. While business prosperity is accompanied by an increase of alcoholism for both whites and Negroes, it is also accompanied by a decrease in homicide of whites and an increase in homicide of Negroes. But the variation in alcoholism has little or no relationship with the variation in homicide either of whites or Negroes. Since both vary independently with the business cycle, the spurious relationship they have with each other disappears when the effect of business fluctuation is removed.

This conclusion is of considerable importance in the development of our conceptual scheme. The alcoholism hypothesis could be viewed as an alternative to our hypothesis that the relation between homicide and the business cycle is a function of aggressive reaction to frustration generated by fluctuations in business. Demonstration of the independence of homicide and alcoholism destroys this alternative explanation.

▶ LYNCHING

Lynching is a form of murder. Raper has found a negative relation between lynchings and the value of cotton.[11] It has also been found that members of lynching mobs are generally lower class whites.[12] Lynching is also a special case of murder of a lower status group by a higher status group. That is, compared to their victims, the murderers involved in lynching represent a higher status group.

In the particular situation represented by lynching, groups of whites, who are victims of depression, *feel* that their social and economic well-being is threatened by Negroes. Their aggression is, therefore, directed against Negroes. This may occur regardless of the nature of the event precipitating a given lynching, e.g., murder, rape, or theft. Various writers have pointed out that the events precipitating lynchings are only excuses for the conflict which ultimately would have occurred on virtually any pretext. The negative correlation between lynching, a form of homicide committed by white persons, and the business cycle strengthens our finding that homicide by white persons, as indexed by cause of death data, correlates negatively with the business cycle.

▶ HOMICIDE BY SEX

Cause of death data cannot be used to differentiate between homicides committed by males and females. Unfortunately, for our purposes, there exists no tendency for males to kill males and for females to kill females. The majority of both male and female homicide victims are killed by males. An attempt has been made, therefore, to seek other data.

Beginning in 1926, the Census Bureau published annual reports of the number of prisoners in State and Federal prisons and reformatories.[13] These volumes also report the number of admissions to penal institutions during a given year, by various population groupings in the United States. Two deficiencies render difficult use of these data for our purposes, viz., (1) continuous series from 1926-41 by sex are not broken down by age, marital status, etc., thus limiting the number of possible correlational comparisons; and (2) exactly the same states do not report each year. The latter difficulty cannot be overcome by standardizing the reporting area, since breakdowns by population groupings are not always given by states.

In spite of these difficulties, we have utilized the series of males and females admitted to state and federal prisons and reformatories for the years 1926-41. The correlation between homicide of *males* admitted to state and federal prisons and reformatories and the business cycle is 0.01, as compared to a coefficient of correlation of 0.15 for the series of females.[14] These correlations, and their differences, are small. The differences are in the direction predicted by our hypothesis, however. Homicide of lower status females may have a stronger positive correlation with the business cycle than homicide of males who hold a relatively higher position in the status hierarchy.

▶ SUMMARY

We have shown that homicide, in contrast with suicide, correlates positively with the business cycle. Further, the positive correlation between homicide and the business cycle cannot be explained as a resultant of the increase in alcoholism during prosperity.

As we move down the status scale, from whites to Negroes, the correlation of homicide with the business cycle changes direction. It is strongly negative for the higher status white category but strongly positive for the subordinate Negro group. In addition, there is tentative evidence that homicide of the lower status female category has a stronger positive correlation with the business cycle than homicide of males enjoying a relatively higher position in the status hierarchy. Lynchings—murders of Negroes by lower class whites—are negatively correlated with the business cycle, lending additional support to our finding that homicide of white persons correlates negatively rather than positively with the business cycle.

An attempted synthesis of our findings on suicide and homicide as they relate to status and the business cycle is presented in the following chapter.

▶ INTRODUCTION

Suicide and the business cycle.—We have shown that suicide of high status categories is more sensitive to fluctuations of the business cycle than suicide of low status categories. Suicide rates of males, whites, the young and middle-aged and those with high income have higher negative correlations with the business cycle than suicide rates of females, Negroes, those beyond age 65, and those with low incomes.

Durkheim's suggestion that abrupt speculative increases in the business cycle were accompanied by increases in the suicide rate fails to be supported since (1) the increase in suicide during the final pre-peak phase of business expansion is more marked for females than for males and (2) years with the most "abrupt" increase in the business index were years of persistent decline in the suicide rate.

Suicide of females tends to reach its peak prior to the business cycle trough. This pattern does not hold for suicide of males which reaches its high point in the same year in which business reaches its low point.

Homicide and the business cycle.—We have shown in Chapter III that homicide, in contrast with suicide, correlates positively

54

with the business cycle and that this relationship cannot be explained by the increase in alcoholism during prosperity. As we move down the status scale from white to Negro, the correlation between homicide and the business cycle changes direction. It is strongly negative for the upper status white group but strongly positive for the subordinate Negro group. There is tentative evidence that homicide of females has a stronger positive correlation with the business cycle than homicide of males. Lynchings—murders of Negroes by lower-class whites—are negatively correlated with the business cycle, lending additional support to our finding that homicide by white persons correlates negatively rather than positively with the business cycle.

▶ INTERPRETATION

Data are introduced in Part II to show that suicide is concentrated in the high status categories of American society while homicide is concentrated in the low status categories. On the basis of these data, let us assume (1) that within each gross ascribed status category,[1] persons who commit suicide are high status persons and persons who commit homicide are low status persons within the category. With this initial assumption, let us examine the hypothesis that both suicide and homicide are extreme forms of aggressive response to frustration, undifferentiated with respect to their source in frustration.

Clinical investigations of the psychoanalysts have suggested that suicide is aggression directed against the self. Both Menninger[2] and Fenichel[3] see suicide as the end of an unfulfilled wish to murder another person. Dollard, Doob, Miller, Mowrer and Sears suggest the "most dramatic form of self-aggression is suicide. . . . It is interesting to note in connection with the assumption that economic depressions increase the average level of frustration of the general population, that Thomas has found the suicide rate to be higher during depression than prosperity."[4]

In stating the frustration-aggression hypothesis, the same authors assume as a point of departure that "aggression is always a consequence of frustration,"[5] and define frustration as "that condition which exists when a goal response suffers interference."[6] Goal response is further defined as that "reaction which reduces the strength of instigation to a degree at which it no longer has as much of a tendency to produce the predicted behavior sequence."[7]

Let us assume (2) that the relevant goal response is the maintenance of a constant or rising position in a status hierarchy relative to the status position of others in the same status reference system. Then let us examine our hypothesis that the acts of both suicide and homicide are undifferentiated responses to extreme frustration arising from extreme loss of position in the status hierarchy relative to the status position of others in the same status reference system. The similarity of this assumption to the "relative deprivation" hypothesis and reference group theory is clear.[8] If group A compares itself with group B and is anxious to maintain or increase its status position relative to group B, forces lowering the status position of group A *relative* to group B should produce frustrations in group A. This would be true, even though the status position of both groups might be rising although at a different rate. Both groups must, of course, be operating in the same status reference system if this type of relative "loss" of status is to produce frustration.

By defining frustration in terms of loss of status position relative to others in the same status reference system, we will very tentatively suggest that high status categories lose status position relative to low status categories during business contraction while low status categories lose status position relative to high status categories during business expansion.

This tentative formulation was first suggested to us by the well-supported fact that females fared better than males, with respect to employment during the depression of the early nineteen thirties in the United States. Stouffer and Lazarsfeld have summarized the statistical data derived from a wide variety of divergent sources leading to this generalization.[9] The upper ascriptive category, males, experienced a higher percentage of unemployment than the lower ascriptive category with which they are compared. The depression increase in the ratio of "additional workers" in the labor market provides further indirect evidence of the *relative* gain in status of the usually non-employed subordinate ascriptive categories.[10]

The problem is complicated by the lack of data for individual cases. We do not know, for example, whether the increase in suicide during business contraction is accounted for by suicide of persons who suffer loss of status by virtue of complete loss of income or whether the increase is accounted for by persons who suffer only partial loss of income. If suicide is a reaction to extreme frustration, it seems probable that frustration would be generated by extreme downward mobility relative to others in the same status reference system. We would expect, therefore, that a person suffering greater downward mobility during business contraction than the average downward mobility of his reference category would experience the greatest frustration. It is true that certain members of all status categories suffer complete loss of income during business contraction. If further research should show that persons with relatively complete loss of income account for the increase in suicide during depression, the intensity of frustration suffered by these persons may vary positively with former status position or with the amount of income lost.

It may be argued that a person who loses all of a $10,000 yearly income during business contraction suffers a greater loss of status relative to others in his reference system than a person who loses all of a $2,000 income during business contraction. A person with little income to begin with may suffer little or no frustration with its loss. Furthermore, if he compares his state with that of others higher in the status hierarcy, he may actually experience a gain in status relative to others when he sees that others who formerly had much higher positions are now reduced to *his* state.

Let us consider two groups at extremes of the American status hierarchy, the high income white and the low income Negro. Let us assume further that each group has certain members who lose all of their income during business contraction. Clearly, members of the high status group will suffer a greater loss than members of the low status group. The loss in status relative to the reference group—and the consequent assumed frustration—will be more severe for members of the high status category than for members of the low status category. The members of the high status group who are reduced to poverty and relief also lose their favored position with respect to the low status group. The distinctions between the races become blurred when there are representatives of each in the bread lines.

If this analysis is proved correct by later research, it would suggest that members of high status groups who suffer complete economic deprivation during business contraction lose status relative to the position of lower status categories while members of the lower status categories gain status with reference to the position of higher status categories.

Our data show that suicide of high ascriptive categories is more sensitive to business contraction than suicide of low ascriptive categories. The foregoing would suggest that complete loss of income by members of high ascriptive categories represents a greater extreme of frustration than complete loss of income by members of lower ascriptive categories. If suicide in response to the business cycle can be accounted for by frustrations generated by loss of status relative to others in the same reference system, it follows that suicide of the high ascriptive categories should be more sensitive than suicide of the low ascriptive categories and our empirical result could be tentatively rationalized.

The correlation of suicide with the business cycle is highly negative for all ascriptive categories as compared with the correlation of homicide and the business cycle. And we have noted that data are presented in Part II showing that suicide is concentrated in the high ascriptive categories while homicide is concentrated in the low ascriptive categories.

If suicide and homicide are acts of aggression undifferentiated with respect to their common source in frustration and if persons who commit suicide are of higher status, on the average, than persons who commit homicide, the argument presented to rationalize the greater sensitivity of suicide of high ascriptive categories as compared with suicide of low ascriptive categories will also rationalize the greater sensitivity of suicide to business contraction as compared with the sensitivity of homicide. Complete loss of income by high status persons—those who commit suicide in response to frustration—represents a greater extreme of frustration than complete loss of income by low status persons—those who commit homicide in response to frustration.

We may subject our formulation to an additional test by consideration of differences in the response of homicide of the white and Negro categories to contraction in business. We have shown that suicide—an act committed by high status persons—is more sensitive to business contraction than homicide—an act committed by low status persons. Further, we have shown that suicide committed by members of high ascriptive categories is more sensitive to business contraction than suicide committed by members of low ascriptive categories. Our data showing that homicide committed by members of high ascriptive categories is more sensitive to business contraction than homicide committed by members of low ascriptive categories provides further support for our tentative formulation.

While homicide of white persons increases during business contraction, homicide of Negroes decreases. From the general negative relation between homicide rates and status position, we assume that persons committing homicide within the white ascriptive category are low status whites while persons committing homicide within the Negro ascriptive category are low status Negroes.

Lynching data suggests that lower class Negroes are in competition with lower class whites for jobs and living space and operate in the same status reference system, i.e., the status of each is defined relative to the status of the other. Lynchings are murders of Negroes by lower class whites and increase during business contraction. If it is true that lower class whites and lower class Negroes are operating in the same status reference system and if the upper ascriptive category—the poor whites—lose position relative to the lower ascriptive category—the lower class Negroes—during business contraction, downward mobility during business contraction would again represent more extreme frustration for members of the upper ascriptive white category than for members of the lower ascriptive Negro category.

In summary, two aspects of our data relating homicide and the business cycle are congruent with our assumption that extreme frustration arises from loss of status relative to the position of others in the same reference system. The fact that lynchings increase during depression suggests that lower class whites and lower class Negroes are operating in the same status reference system and that the status differential between the groups decreases during business contraction. The fact that homicide of lower class whites is more sensitive to business contraction than homicide of lower class Negroes is congruent with our formulation that the whites would suffer the greatest frustration from their loss of position with reference to the Negro group with which they compare themselves.

If this analysis is correct, it would suggest that the same forces which *increase* frustration during business contraction for lower class whites should *decrease* frustration during business contraction for lower class Negroes. The data conform with this suggestion. Homicide of Negroes does decrease during business contraction. With the gain in status relative to the position of the lower class whites during business contraction, frustration of Negroes and their homicide rate decreases.

When data through time on rates of Negro homicide by class become available, this formulation could be subjected to rigorous test. For example, it suggests that homicide by upper class Negroes would increase and that homicide by lower class Negroes would decrease during business contraction. While lower class Negroes tend to compare their lot with that of the poor whites, upper class Negroes tend to compare themselves with lower class Negroes rather than with members of the white category. Drake and Cayton note that upper class Negroes are "almost completely absorbed in the social ritual (within the Negro community) and in the struggle to 'get ahead.' Both these goals are inextricably bound up with 'advancing the Race' and with civic leadership. In actuality, the Negro upper-class way of life is a substitute for complete integration into the general American society, but it has compensations of its own which allow individuals to gain social stability and inner satisfactions, despite the conditions in the Black Ghetto and their rejection by white America."[11] Drake and Cayton also point out that the Negro upper class in "Black Metropolis" consists largely of business and professional groupings, a situation resulting from segregation which creates petty monopolies and operates to the advantage of members of the upper class community.

We should expect the upper class Negro to suffer loss of position relative to the status position of lower class Negroes during business contraction in much the same way in which lower class whites suffer loss of position relative to the status position of the lower class Negro. Our suicide data further suggest that upper class Negroes do not define their status position with reference to that of upper class whites in the way in which lower class Negroes define their position with reference to that of lower class whites. It is probable that position within the Negro community is the important referent for the upper class Negro while position with respect to the lower class white is the important status referent for the lower class Negro.

Our tentative formulation of suicide and homicide as acts of aggression undifferentiated with respect to their common source in frustrations arising from loss of status relative to others in the same status reference system would be more convincing if it could also account for the rise in homicide among Negroes during business expansion. This fact would be congruent with our formulation if we could show why lower class Negroes would be subject to extreme loss of status relative to others in their status reference system when business conditions were improving. If our assumptions are correct, Negroes who commit homicide rank at the bottom of our hierarchy of status since they are lower class members of our lowest ascriptive category. We have suggested that they do not suffer frustration specifically as a result of business fluctuations during business contraction because their position at the bottom of the status hierarchy makes it impossible for them to lose status relative to the status position of others in their reference system. The difference between the position of a lower class Negro with no income and the position of a lower class Negro with income equal to the average of his category is very slight, as are the consequences to him of complete loss of his income. Our lynching data have suggested that business contraction narrows the status gap between lower class Negroes and their major reference group—the lower class whites. If poor whites have more to lose with business contraction than lower class Negroes, the poor whites suffer a loss in status relative to the lower class Negroes and the Negroes experience a gain in status with reference to the lower class whites. The situation reverses with business expansion and the widening of the status gap between the two groups. The caste system operates to give whites a disproportionate share of the increasing job opportunities. Negroes are hired only after the white demand for jobs is filled. Color caste restricts the degree to which Negroes are able to take advantage of the opportunities provided by expanding business. White persons suffer no such restrictions. As the gap between the two groups in the same status reference system widens, Negroes suffer a loss in status relative to the whites while the whites experience a gain in status relative to the Negroes. With our assumption that frustration varies with the change in status relative to others in the same reference system, frustration of the poor whites would decrease with business expansion while frustration of the lower class Negroes would increase. If the variation in homicide with the business cycle (as well as the variation in suicide with the business cycle) indexes the variation in frustration suffered by differing status categories, our empirical result that homicide of whites falls while homicide of Negroes rises with expanding business would be congruent with our over-all formulation.

We have shown that the increase in suicide just prior to the peak of the business cycle noted by Durkheim is more characteristic of suicide of females than of suicide of males and have used this finding to question the validity of one portion of Durkheim's formulation of suicide. Our formulation in terms of the frustration-aggression hypothesis provides a tentative alternative. If we are correct in assuming that frustration increases with loss of status relative to the position of others in the same reference system, the tendency for frustration of females to increase during the final phase of business expansion may be due to the relative exclusion of females from participation in the speculative gain characteristic of this phase of prosperity. The world of speculative finance is largely a male world. If the increase in female suicide prior to the peak of business should turn out to reflect suicide of women losing ground in the competition with men for the rewards of prosperity, our analysis would suggest that frustration might accrue from their loss of position relative to that of men who were rising in status at a more rapid rate. The same factor may be operating on the other low ascriptive categories. Subordinate status position acts to limit the probability of maximizing economic gain during business expansion for all low ascriptive categories. The upward mobility of females and the aged is restricted by their relative exclusion from the labor market. Lower income groups are limited by their lack of capital and Negroes are limited by their color. But the intensity of the "status" block to upward mobility increases with the degree of subordination and reaches sufficient force to produce frustration during business expansion only among lower class Negroes at the very bottom of the status hierarchy.

We have seen that suicide of whites is more sensitive to the fluctuations of business than suicide of Negroes and have interpreted the difference as a function of the greater frustration imposed by business contraction on upper class members of the white ascriptive category as compared with upper class members of the Negro ascriptive category. If the upper class Negro and the upper class white were operating in the same reference system, consistency would require that we predict a positive rather than a negative correlation between suicide of Negroes and the business cycle. But the data showing that the correlations are negative are consistent with the observation noted above that upper class Negroes tend to define their status with reference to lower class members of the Negro community rather than with reference to members of the white community.

One of the components of status position is income and economists have done some work on the effect of the business cycle on income distribution.[12] Mendershausen has shown that income dispersion in dollar terms declines with the drop in mean income during periods of business contraction, and increases with the rise in mean income during periods of business expansion. Standard deviations of the income distribution drop consistently between 1929 and 1933.[13] Mendershausen has compared the effect of the depression on high and low income groups in 1929.

When 1929 is the base year, the recipients of very low and of moderately high incomes in 1929 fare relatively well during the depression, while those with moderately low and extremely high incomes fare relatively ill. The positive deviations of the recipients of moderately high 1929 incomes can be explained by the relative stability of salary and high wage incomes, the negative deviations of the moderately low and top incomes, by the strong incidence of unemployment among the former, and by the effect of falling property income, in particular income from dividends and speculative gains, among the latter.[14]

It is probable that the very low incomes in 1929 were concentrated in the low status Negro group while the very high incomes were concentrated in the high status white group. It is worthy of note that our formulation suggests that the highest income group which "fared relatively ill" during the depression suffered the maximum frustration during business contraction while the lowest income group which fared "relatively well" suffered the minimum frustration during business contraction.

The highly tentative interpretations presented in this chapter suggest the reasonableness of our hypothesis that suicide and homicide are acts of aggression undifferentiated with respect to their common source in frustration generated by business cycles. Certain of the earlier explanations of correlations of suicide and homicide with the business cycle have been questioned. The association between homicide and alcoholism cannot account for the relation of homicide with the business cycle. Nor can the Durkheim formulation based on variation in the control of social norms over behavior account for the persistent negative correlations between suicide and the business cycle.

Our argument based on the frustration-aggression hypothesis and the clinical formulation of suicide as a form of aggression has attempted to tie together into a more or less coherent whole the disparate correlations of both suicide and homicide with the business cycle and tentatively explain them as aggressive reactions to frustration generated by differential changes in status position accompanying the ebb and flow of economic forces. It will require much further research before the adequacy of our formulation can be tested. A number of specific projects designed for this purpose are suggested in the final chapter.

In Part II we take as our starting point the assumption that both suicide and homicide are acts of aggression undifferentiated with respect to their source in frustration. We will seek instead the determinants of the target of the aggression and raise this question: Why does one person react to frustration by turning the resultant aggression against someone else while another person reacts to frustration by turning the resultant aggression against himself?

part two

SOME SOCIOLOGICAL

DETERMINANTS OF THE CHOICE

BETWEEN SUICIDE AND HOMICIDE

In this chapter, a very tentative attempt is made to reduce the known sociological correlates of suicide to two variable and suggest a common element uniting them.

The assumptions and hypotheses presented in this chapter are derived from examination of the *absolute* rates of suicide at a given point in time, not from *variation* in rates of suicide through time. Part I dealt with variation in rates through time. Confusion between the formulations of Part I and those presented in this chapter derived from study of differences in absolute rates of suicide at the same point in time should be avoided.

The theoretical view of Durkheim that subordinate status position operates to reduce the probability of suicide because of the restraint enforced by the subordinate status is clearly evident in the following quotation:

The enormous rate of those with independent means . . . sufficiently shows that the possessors of most comfort suffer most. Everything that enforces subordination attenuates the effects of this state. At least the horizon of the lower classes is limited by those above them, and for this same reason their desires are more modest. Those who have only empty space above them are almost invariably lost in it, if no force restrains them. . . .[1]

These statements include three elements: an hypothesis; an assumption; and a postulate. The hypothesis predicts a positive relation between suicide and position in a status hierarchy which may be stated as follows: high status categories, other things being equal, will have higher suicide rates than low status categories.

The assumption: high status categories, by virtue of their high status, are subjected to fewer external restraints than low status categories which are subject to restraints imposed by groups higher in the status hierarchy.

The postulate: suicide rates in high status categories are greater than suicide rates in low status categories *because* high status categories are subject to fewer external restraints than low status categories.

Let us accept as an assumption that high status categories are subject to fewer external restraints than low status categories and test the hypothesis that high status categories will have higher suicide rates than low status categories. If the hypothesis is denied, the postulate that suicide rates in high status categories are greater *because* high status categories are subjected to fewer external restraints will also be denied. But if the hypothesis is confirmed, the postulate will be neither confirmed nor denied and we will be forced to go to further observations for its confirmation or rejection.

Absolute rates of suicide of groups in differing levels of the status hierarchy were examined as a preliminary test of the hypothesis.

Let us make five assumptions about the position of broad status categories in the status hierarchy in the United States.

1. As status categories, white persons in the United States rank higher than Negroes.
2. As status categories, males in the United States rank higher than females.
3. As status categories, high income groups rank higher than low income groups.
4. As status categories, the young and middle aged rank higher than those past the age of 65.
5. As status categories, United States Army officers rank higher than United States Army enlisted men.[2]

The criteria used in the rankings by race, sex, income and age have been treated in Chapter II. The distinction between commissioned and enlisted military personnel is based on a rigid hierarchical ranking.

All of these assumptions are presented very tentatively. We are required to use these gross categories because they are the only ones for which suicide data are available. The rough hierarchical rankings are necessary in our attempt to isolate certain of the important correlates of suicide in the "theory building" stage of research. If this procedure is successful in generating hypotheses which are testable on more refined data, the tentative quality of assumptions made in the early stages will be justified.

With these assumptions, we may compare the absolute suicide rates of whites and Negroes, of males and females, of the young and the aged, among high and low income groups, and among Army officers and enlisted men, providing five tests of the hypothesis.

White persons in the United States have about three times as high a suicide rate as Negroes and males have a rate about three times as high as females. The weight of the evidence as assessed by Dublin and Bunzel is that suicide predominates primarily at the top of the socio-economic scale. In 12 of the 16 years between 1914 and 1929, officers in the Army had a higher rate than enlisted men.

Granting our initial assumptions, in four of the five cases of comparison, categories with the higher status have higher absolute rates of suicide than categories with the lower status.

The case of age is the important exception. Although we have accepted Dublin and Bunzel's assessment of the data on socio-economic status, additional data from Chicago show that the suicide rate is higher in the low rent community areas of Chicago than it is in the high rent areas, providing another exception to the over-all pattern.

The low status group aged 65-74 years has about two and one-half times as high a suicide rate as the status group aged 25-34 and the residents of low status low rent community areas in Chicago have nearly one and one-half times as high a suicide rate as residents of the high status high rent areas.

While the bulk of the evidence seems to confirm the hypothesis that suicide is primarily concentrated in high status groupings, these two cases are contradictory.

Let us assume for the present that the higher *absolute* rates of suicide of the aged as compared with the young, and of residents of low rental areas as compared with residents of high rental areas are functions of some second unknown factor and return to the assumption derived from Durkheim that high status categories, by virtue of their high status, are subjected to fewer external restraints than low status categories which are subject to restraints imposed by groups higher in the status hierarchy.

With this assumption, and the very tentative acceptance of the hypothesis that high status categories will have higher rates than low status categories, we are unable to deny the postulate derived from Durkheim, i.e., that suicide rates in high status categories are greater than suicide rates in low status categories *because* high status categories are subject to fewer external restraints than low status categories. Our postulate would be strengthened if the incorporation of our assumed unknown variable into the theory (a) provided a tentative rationale for our two contradictory cases, together with other correlates of suicide largely independent of status, and (b) proved to be another form of external control. Let us turn now to our assumption of the existence of this second variable.

Durkheim and the theorists of social and personal disorganization have postulated relationships between suicide and the degree of participation in group relationships.

Durkheim, in his concept of egoistic suicide first called attention to the significance of "truly collective activity" for suicide.

. . . Both (anomic and egoistic suicide) spring from society's insufficient presence in individuals. But the sphere of its absence is not the same in both cases. In egoistic suicide it is deficient in truly collective activity, thus depriving the latter of object and meaning. . . .[3]

Durkheim's three propositions, derived from his empirical observations of the operation of egoistic suicide focus, in a parallel way, on suicide as a function of the degree of integration of the society.

Suicide varies inversely with the degree of integration of religious society.
Suicide varies inversely with the degree of integration of domestic society.
Suicide varies inversely with the degree of integration of political society.[4]

Let us assume that our unknown variable is defined as the "degree of involvement of an individual in relationships with other persons." Further, postulate that the probability of suicide varies inversely with the degree of involvement of an individual in relationships with other persons.

The following assumption is made at this point to generate a testable hypothesis relating to this postulate.

Assumption: the degree of involvement in relationships with other persons is greater, on the average, for the married category than for the single, the widowed, or the divorced categories.

Hypothesis: the suicide rate of the married will be lower than the suicide rates of the single, the widowed, or the divorced.

Test of the hypothesis: the suicide rate per 100,000 married persons in the United States in 1940 was 18.0. Rates of 30.9 for the widowed and 64.3 for the divorced are greater than the rate for the married and the difference is in the expected direction. The rate of 6.8 for single persons, however, is lower than the rate for the married and contradicts the hypothesis. Replication of the test, holding sex constant, reveals the same pattern of variation in suicide rates by marital status.

We know, however, that marital status varies with age. By holding age constant, the contradiction turns out to be a spurious function of this relation between marital status and age.

For each age grouping over age 20, the suicide rate of married persons is lower than the suicide rate of single persons in the same age group. This pattern of variation holds up for both males and females with only one exception.[5]

Our observations confirm the hypothesis that the suicide rate of the married is lower than the suicide rate of the single, the widowed, or the divorced.

If our assumption is true, i.e., that the degree of involvement in relationships with other persons is greater for the married than for the single, widowed and divorced categories, confirmation of the hypothesis that suicide is lower for the married than for the other categories gives empirical weight to our postulate stating that the probability of suicide varies inversely with the degree of involvement of an individual in relationships with other persons.

Let us turn now to consideration of another quotation of Durkheim in his discussion of egoistic suicide.

The more weakened the groups to which he belongs, the less he depends on them, the more he consequently depends only on himself and recognizes no other rules of conduct than what are founded on his private interests. If we agree to call this state egoism, in which the individual ego asserts itself to excess in the face of the social ego and at its expense, we may call egoistic the special type of suicide springing from excessive individualism.

But how can suicide have such an origin?

First of all, it can be said that, as collective force is one of the obstacles best calculated to restrain suicide, its weakening involves a development of suicide.[6]

Durkheim uses the words "collective force" to describe the effects of involvement in relationships on the probability of suicide. The weakening of these relationships—this "collective force"—is seen as leading to suicide.

The theorists of social and personal disorganization have treated suicide as a function of the weakening of social controls over behavior.

Weber has defined the term "social relationship" to denote "the behavior of a plurality of actors insofar as, in its meaningful content, the action of each takes account of that of the others and is oriented in these terms." If the action of each "takes account of that of the others," the behavior of one party to a "social" relationship must, by definition, suffer some degree of restraint to make it conform to the wishes and expectations of the other party to the relationship.[7]

Let us assume: (1) that present in every "social" or "cathectic" relationship is an element of restraint which acts to curb action or behavior of parties to the relationship; (2) that this element arises directly out of the relationship and is external to the personalities of the individuals who are a party to the relationship; (3) that acceptance of the element of restraint by each party to the relationship is a condition of the continuation of the relationship.

Let us define the degree of involvement in "cathectic" relationships with other persons as "strength of the relational system" and re-state our hypothesis as follows: the probability of suicide varies inversely with the strength of the relational system of the individual.

Persons with strong relational systems are, by definition, subjected to greater external restraints than persons with weak relational systems. If we are correct in assuming that the relational systems of married persons are stronger than the relational systems of the single, widowed and divorced categories, we have initial evidence on the validity of the following postulate.

Postulate: The probability of suicide varies inversely with the strength of the relational system *because* persons with strong relational systems are subjected to greater external restraints than persons with weak relational systems.

Two major postulates have emerged from our work, both positing an inverse relationship between external restraints and suicide. Postulate (1) states that suicide rates in high status categories are higher than suicide rates in low status categories *because* high status categores are subject to fewer external restraints than low status categories.

Postulate (2) states that the probability of suicide varies inversely with the strength of the relational system *because* persons with strong relational systems are subjected to greater external restraints than persons with weak relational systems.

Our first postulate includes within it the statement of a positive relationship between position in a status hierarchy and suicide. The reader will remember that five tests of this relationship were presented. The hypothesis held up for the categories of race, sex, Army rank, and income, but was denied when tested on age. We have suggested a second variable and have called it the "strength of the relational system" and have assumed that it varies with marital status.

Both of these variables of status position and strength of relational system have been related conceptually to the degree of external restraint imposed on behavior.

Let us return now to our hypothesis of a positive relation between suicide and position in a status hierarchy. A contradiction to the general pattern was the higher suicide rate of the age groupings beyond 65. We had assumed that the older age categories suffer a decline in status and had ranked them lower in a hierarchy of status than the younger age groupings. With this assumption, we would expect the suicide rate to be lower in the age groups past 65 rather than higher as is actually the case.

Let us examine two other striking sociological correlates of suicide before we attempt to rationalize the empirical data on age. Residents of urban areas in the United States have higher suicide rates than residents of rural areas. In 1940, the suicide rate per 100,000 was 16.8 in cities over 100,000 population, 15.6 in cities between 10,000 and 100,000, 15.1 in cities 2,500 to 10,000 and 12.0 in rural areas. The same pattern holds up when race is held constant.

Cavan and Schmid, in their studies of the ecological distribution of suicide in American cities, found a concentration of suicide in the disorganized central sectors of cities.[8] The high rates found in the "skid row" sections of cities were interpreted as resulting from the ineffective control of social norms over behavior in these areas. Vice, prostitution and delinquency were also prevalent in these "disorganized" areas.

One of the critical differences between rural and urban life is in the stability and continuity of family life. The strong control exercised by the community or neighborhood on the farm or in the small town contrasts sharply with the anonymity and impersonality of life in the city. The urban family is subjected to disrupting forces largely absent in rural areas. These characteristics of the big city are magnified in the skid row areas of homeless men. Life in the rooming house sections of Chicago, for example, reaches an extreme in anonymity and residential turnover. Behavior is free from the need for conformity to the demands and expectations of others because "others" do not care.

The foregoing suggests that the high suicide rates in cities as compared with rural areas, and in the central disorganized sectors of cities as compared with outlying residential districts may reflect urban-rural differences in the degree of involvement of persons in meaningful relationships with other persons.

If further research should confirm the available data showing variation in strength of the relational system in urban and rural areas, and in integrated and disorganized areas within cities, the empirical findings of urban-rural and ecological variations in suicide may be classed theoretically with the relation between suicide and marital status. Categories with low suicide rates—the married, residents of rural areas, and residents of integrated and organized urban communities—are all categories with strong relational systems as compared with the comparable high suicide categories—the unmarried, residents of cities, and inhabitants of high mobility areas of rooming houses and homeless men.

We have shown how the urban-rural and ecological effects on suicide may be interpreted in terms of our second variable, the strength of the relational system. This formulation adds further confirmation to the postulate that suicide varies inversely with the strength of the relational system because persons with strong relational systems are subjected to greater external restraints than persons with weak relational systems.

Let us now return to the relation between suicide and age which contradicted our prediction that the drop in status beyond age 65 would lower the suicide rate in the older age categories. The reader will remember that in our other four cases, the low status categories had lower suicide rates than the higher status categories with which they were compared. We had noted that our postulate that suicide varies positively with status because high status categories are subject to fewer external restraints would be strengthened if the other correlates of suicide could be rationalized as another form of external restraint. We have shown that the relation between suicide and marital status, suicide and place of residence, and suicide and urban ecology can be viewed as a function of a second form of external restraint over behavior—the type imposed by virtue of involvement in cathectic relationships with other persons.

The hypothesis that the strength of the relational system decreases with age is presented very tentatively in an attempt to rationalize the relation between suicide and age in a manner congruent with our theoretical formulation. This hypothesis states that the degree of involvement in cathectic relationships with other persons decreases with increasing age.

The increase of suicide with age cannot be attributed solely to change in the size of the "family of pro-creation" since it occurs for all categories when marital status is held constant. But the degree of involvement in cathectic relationships with the "family of orientation" does vary with age simply as a function of parental mortality.

Figure 1 shows the suicide rate of white males and the percent of paternal orphans, both plotted against age. Two things should be noted: (1) suicide of white males and the probability of having a deceased father both rise sharply with age; (2) both curves level off after age 55-64 when the suicide rate remains relatively constant as does the 1.0 probability of having a deceased father. Clearly, the fact that the two curves rise together does not mean that there is any relationship between suicide and the percentage of orphans.[9] Demonstration of this hypothesis derived from our theoretical argument must await research on the incidence of suicide among orphans as compared with non-orphans. We suggest, nevertheless, that the presence or absence of parents is an important element in the variable of strength of the relational system and that this element varies with age in much the same way as the suicide rate.

European data show that parenthood operates to reduce the suicide rate, particularly of females and it is certainly true that the presence of children operates as more of a "restraint" on the mother than on the father. As the parents age, the children grow up and leave the home thus weakening the strength of the relational system and reducing the "restraint" imposed on the parents. Data on the number of children living in the home, together with data on parental survival may explain the marked effect of age upon the suicide rate.

Data are not available to test these formulations but they are suggested here as a set of theoretically derived hypotheses which can be tested and which will when tested provide either strong confirmation or strong denial of our theoretical formulation. In a later chapter data are presented showing that homicide, in contrast with suicide, is concentrated in the younger age categories. Since our final formulation suggests that suicide varies negatively with the strength of external restraint over behavior while homicide varies positively with the strength of external restraint, empirical study of our hypothesis about age will provide a test of one of the corner stones of the social-psychological theory of violence developed in this volume.

Let us briefly summarize our argument thus far. Our two postulates, one derived from the relation between suicide and position in the status hierarchy, the other derived from the relation between suicide and the strength of the relational system, posit a negative relation between the strength of external restraints on behavior and suicide.

Percent of
persons with
deceased fathers

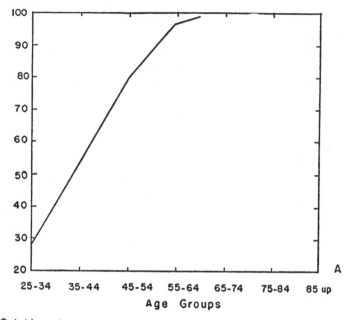

Suicide rate
per 100,000

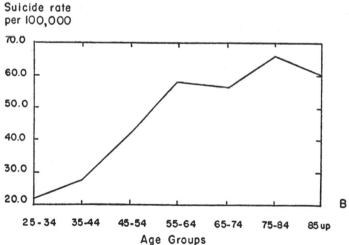

Figure 1. Suicide, Paternal Mortality and Age. Suicide of White Males,
U.S.D.R.S., 1940 Increases with Age in Much the Same Way as Does
the Probability of Having a Deceased Father.

We have grouped the correlates of suicide in two variables, position in a status hierarchy and degree of relational involvement with other persons. We have further deduced a common element of these two variables which we have labelled external restraint.

Behavior of subordinate status groups is restrained by the weight of the demands and expectations imposed by other groups higher in the status hierarchy. Behavior of the Negro is subject to the demands of white persons to a greater extent than behavior of the white person is subject to the demands of Negroes. The behavior of an employee is subject to greater restraint than behavior of his superior. Power is associated with status position and this is recognized by both parties to the relationship, subordinate and superordinate. But it is the behavior of the subordinate which must conform to the expectations of his superior. The superior is not similarly limited. Let us label the type of external restraint varying with the position in a status hierarchy as "vertical" restraint. The vertical restraint demanded by subordinate status is of a different order from the restraint demanded as a condition of collective living. Whether a person is of the highest or the lowest status, as long as he is operating in a network of interpersonal relationships, his behavior must also conform to the demands and expectations of other parties to the relationship. And this conformity requires that he restrain his behavior. He must control and modify his impulsive behavior to meet the definitions operating in the relationship. Let us label this type of restraint which varies with the strength of the relational system as "horizontal" restraint.

But whether the restraint derives from subordinate status or from inter-personal relations with other persons, it seems to provide immunity from suicide. This is the tentative conclusion to which we have arrived from our attempt to relate the theory of Durkheim with later empirical studies.

In Chapter VII we will take our argument one step further and attempt to relate our formulation of an inverse relation between suicide and external restraint with the psychoanalytic formulation of suicide by suggesting a tentative integration of the sociological formulation of suicide as a function of too little external restraint over behavior and the psychoanalytic formulation of suicide as a function of too much internal restraint over behavior.

But first let us turn to an examination of the relation between homicide and certain of its sociological correlates. Data bearing upon the relation of homicide with status and of homicide with the strength of the relational system are presented in the next chapter, permitting us to bring together in the same conceptual system acts of violence against the self and acts of violence against another person.

▶ INTRODUCTION

In this Chapter we will examine the relation between homicide, status and the strength of the relational system. The reader will recall that the relationships found between suicide, status and strength of the relational system led us in Chapter V to postulate a negative relation between suicide and the strength of external restraint over behavior. The data which are presented below lead us tentatively to a second postulate of a positive relation between homicide and the strength of external restraint. In the following Chapter, these two postulates are related to certain psychological concepts and to the business cycle as a source of frustration in the formulation of a social-psychological theory of violence.

▶ DATA

Let us assume, as we did in Chapter II, that white persons are of higher status than Negroes, that residents of the highly industrial North are of higher status than residents of the economically depressed South, and that males as a gross category rank higher in the American status hierarchy than females, and let us test the hypothesis that homicide rates are higher in the low status categories and lower in the high status categories.

Cause of death by homicide statistics provide our most reliable comparison of homicide rates of whites and Negroes.[1] There were approximately ten times as many deaths of Negroes by homicide in the United States in 1940 as deaths of white persons by homicide. The rate for "all other races" in the United States in 1940 was 33.3 per 100,000. The rate for white persons was only 3.1 per 100,000. We have presented data elsewhere indicating that the overwhelming majority of murders are committed by members of the same race as the person murdered.

These data show a very much higher homicide rate for the low status Negro category as compared with the rate for higher status whites. The higher homicide rate of Negroes does not appear to be merely a reflection of higher Negro crime rates in general, since Negro rates of homicide and assault are even higher in relation to white rates for these crimes than are rates for other crimes. Sutherland indicates that,

"While 3.1 times as many Negroes as white persons, per 100,000 population, were arrested in 1940 for all types of crimes, 8.6 times as many were arrested for assault, 7.2 times as many for homicide, 4.7 times as many for robbery, 4.2 times as many for larceny, 3.4 times as many for burglary, and 3.0 times as many for rape."[2]

It has long been noted by criminologists that crimes of violence against the person are especially present in the Southern part of this country.[3] Thus, a compilation of "Urban Crime Rates, 1951, by Geographic Divisions and States" reveals the following facts with reference to murder and aggravated assault:[4]

Table 1—Urban Rates of Murder and Aggravated Assault, by Geographic Divisions of the United States, 1951

Geographic Division	Murder Rate	Aggravated Assault Rate
East South Central	12.45	102.6
South Atlantic	10.30	214.9
West South Central	9.11	75.9
East North Central	4.33	66.4
Pacific	3.21	49.7
West North Central	3.05	52.3
Mountain	2.76	36.3
Middle Atlantic	2.56	34.9
New England	1.24	12.1

This regional variation in rates of crimes of violence against the person has usually been explained in terms of the traditions of feuding and lynching in the South and in terms of the large number of Negroes in that section of the country.[5] Regarding the latter point, however, we note with Sutherland that "homicides, at least, cannot be explained so simply, for the death rate by homicide for white persons in the South is approximately five times as high as in New England. . . ."[6] Negro homicide rates tend also to be lower in the North than in the South.

Table 2 brings together data on white and Negro homicide rates for such states as had Negro and white homicide victims, and stable rates, for the year 1940. These states are grouped according to the broad North-South distinction.

The median of white homicide death rates, from Table 2, is 5.0, the rate of South Carolina and Virginia, two Southern states. All eight Northern states fall below this median, while eight Southern states out of eleven are above it and only one below it. Three of the Border states, including Washington, D. C., are above the median, and three below it.

The median of Negro homicide death rates is 33.5, the rate of Indiana, a Northern state. Five out of eight Northern states fall below this median, only two above it. Five out of eleven Southern states are above the median. Of the Border states, all commonly associated with "the South," only Maryland is below the median.

The regional variation in crimes of violence against the person conforms with our hypothesis that low status groups have higher homicide rates than higher status groups. The economically depressed South reacts to poverty and a generally lower socio-economic status with higher homicide rates than the highly industrialized states of the North.

Porterfield has recently noted that "in Southern cities, with some exceptions, crime rates are higher and suicide rates lower than in non-Southern cities paired with the former. Since the latter tend to be relatively high in socio-economic status and the former relatively low, it turns out that higher suicide rates appear in cities with higher, not the lower status."[7] Uniform Crime Reports indicate, however, that the Southern states do not have the highest rates in the country for crimes against property, indicating that the North-South differential is accounted for primarily by crimes against persons.[8] Porterfield's conclusion is of particular interest to our theory. He finds that "areas with high suicide and low crime rates are high in social status . . . ," and "areas of low suicide and high crime rates have low scores for social status. . . ."[9]

Table 2—Number of Deaths from Homicide per 100,000 Population, by State and Race, 1940[a]

		RACE
States	White	All Other
NORTH		
California	3.9	24.8
Illinois	2.6	42.5
Indiana	2.2	33.5
Michigan	1.9	28.6
New Jersey	1.6	15.3
New York	2.0	20.2
Ohio	2.6	43.4
Pennsylvania	1.9	22.2
SOUTH		
Alabama	6.9	34.4
Arkansas	5.1	24.6
Florida	7.5	59.4
Georgia	5.6	47.1
Louisiana	5.5	23.6
Mississippi	5.7	28.7
North Carolina	4.0	28.3
South Carolina	5.0	24.0
Tennessee	7.1	61.5
Texas	5.3	35.4
Virginia	5.0	27.2
BORDER		
Kentucky	10.4	61.6
Maryland	2.8	32.4
Missouri	2.9	42.4
Oklahoma[b]	3.2	35.3
Washington, D. C.[c]	5.3	35.0
West Virginia[d]	5.4	54.3

a. Source: United States Department of Commerce, Bureau of the Census, *Vital Statistics Rates in the United States, 1900-1940,* (Washington: Government Printing Office, 1943), adapted from Table 20.
b. Indian territory at the time of the Civil War, controlled by the Confederacy.
c. Though the Northern capital during the Civil War, traditionally considered a "Southern" area.
d. Broke off from Virginia during the Civil War.

The following table of death rates from suicide and homicide reveals the tremendous contrast in these rates between the states comprising the East South Central and the South Atlantic states, the two highest divisions with respect to murder and aggravated assault in Table 1, and the states in the New England and Middle Atlantic divisions, which had the lowest rates of murder and aggravated assault.

Table 3—Number of Deaths from Suicide and Homicide per 100,000 Population, for Selected States, 1940*

States	Suicide Death Rates	Homicide Death Rates
NEW ENGLAND		
Connecticut	17.9	1.8
Maine	15.7	1.5
Massachusetts	13.3	1.5
New Hampshire	16.3	1.4
Rhode Island	12.6	1.4
Vermont	16.7	0.8
MIDDLE ATLANTIC		
New Jersey	16.4	2.3
New York	16.7	2.8
Pennsylvania	12.9	2.9
SOUTH ATLANTIC		
Delaware	14.3	4.5
Florida	15.0	21.6
Georgia	9.1	20.0
Maryland	16.3	7.7
North Carolina	8.1	10.8
South Carolina	6.3	13.2
Virginia	14.9	10.5
West Virginia	10.3	8.4
EAST SOUTH CENTRAL		
Alabama	8.3	16.4
Kentucky	10.1	14.3
Mississippi	6.4	17.0
Tennessee	8.8	16.6

* Source: United States Department of Commerce, Bureau of the Census, *Vital Statistics Rates in the United States, 1900-1940,* (Washington: Government Printing Office, 1943), adapted from Table 21.

As we move from North to South in the United States, the probability of suicide decreases as the probability of homicide increases. At the same time, the proportion of Negroes in the total population is increasing with an associated strengthening of the rigidity of color caste. But the fact that rates of homicide remain higher in the economically depressed South than in the higher status North when the effect of race is held constant provides additional verification for our hypothesis that homicide is negatively related to position in the status hierarchy.

The relation between homicide and sex provides the third test of our hypothesis that homicide is inversely related to status. We would predict that homicide rates would be higher for females, the lower status category, than for males.

The facts contradict this prediction. In 1950, according to the Uniform Crime Reports, 5,482 males were arrested for the offense of criminal homicide. Only 854 females were arrested for the same offense in 1950. The same pattern holds up when we examine the distribution of arrests for assault by sex. Over 53,000 males were arrested for this offense as compared with about 6,300 females.[10] Over 7 times as many males as females were arrested for homicide and over 8 times as many males were arrested for assault. The male-female differential is somewhat greater for assault than for homicide.

With very few exceptions, such as homicide of persons under 1 year of age—committed almost exclusively by women—males commit more of all types of crimes than females. But an interesting and important difference between the sexes appears when we examine the number of homicides as a proportion of all crimes committed by each of the sex categories. In 1940, 8.4 per cent of all females committed to state and federal prisons or reformatories were committed for the offense of homicide. Only 4.2 per cent of all males committed were committed for the offense of homicide.[11] This ratio of approximately two to one is maintained over a number of years.[12]

There are two additional factors which may be introduced in an attempt to rationalize this contradiction. We have already noted that the homicide rate among Negroes, our low status category, is about ten times as great as the homicide rate among white persons. Since Negroes make up a disproportionate share of the total number of homicides, the status differentiation between males and females is worth examining. In Chapter II we presented the finding that the suicide rate of Negro females correlated more highly with the business cycle than the suicide rate of Negro males. Since this finding represented the single exception to data showing consistently higher correlations for males than for females, we suggested that it was congruent with the observations of a number of writers that females in the Negro community tend to enjoy a prestige position equal to, if not exceeding that of males.

It is interesting that the same interpretation can be applied in the present contradiction. If it is true that the prestige position of the Negro female is higher, on the average, than the prestige position of the Negro male, we would predict from our hypothesis that the Negro female would have a lower homicide rate than the Negro male.

Data are not available adequately to test this formulation. If it is correct, however, further research should show that the ratio of male to female homicide among Negroes is higher than the ratio of male to female homicide among whites.

One additional "extenuating" factor may be introduced in the interpretation of the contradictory finding with respect to sex. Cultural definitions about the external expression of aggression differ by sex. The culturally-prescribed passivity for females contrasts sharply with the masculine premium on aggressiveness and physical strength.

We had assumed in Chapter V that persons beyond the age of 65 years were of lower status than persons in the younger age categories and were forced to reject the hypothesis that the age category with the highest status would have the highest rate.

We are similarly forced to reject the parallel hypothesis positing higher homicide rates in the older, lower status age categories. Data collected by Frankel are presented in Table 4.[13]

Table 4—Per Cent of Homicides Committed in New Jersey, by Age, Nativity, and Race, 1925-34

Age Group	Total	Native Born White	Foreign Born	Negro
All Ages	100	100	100	100
Under 20 Years	7.9	13.1	3.4	8.1
20-24	18.9	25.6	14.9	16.8
25-29	19.8	23.8	17.8	18.2
30-34	17.5	12.8	19.3	20.2
35-39	12.9	8.7	15.1	14.5
40-44	8.5	4.7	11.0	9.4
45-49	5.5	4.4	6.5	5.4
50-54	4.1	1.6	5.2	5.4
55-59	2.3	2.5	3.1	1.0
60-64	1.7	2.2	2.4	0.3
65 and over	0.9	0.6	1.3	0.7

Additional data are presented in Table 5 in the form of a rough index of homicide and aggravated assault by age groups in the United States.[14]

Beginning with the age group, 20-24, the relation between age and these crimes of violence against the person is clearly negative. Homicide is concentrated in the younger age groupings and is virtually non-existent beyond the age of 65.

In two of our four tests the hypothesis that homicide varies inversely with status is confirmed. In the case of sex, the hypothesis is not confirmed. We have offered several speculative rationalizations

Table 5—Homicides and Aggravated Assaults per 100,000 Population in the United States, by Age—1950*

Age Group	Homicide Rate	Aggravated Assault Rate
All Ages	4.20	39.48
15-19	4.84	39.47
20-24	10.27	101.95
25-29	9.84	99.17
30-34	8.14	83.59
35-39	7.16	67.94
40-44	5.84	54.41
45-49	4.78	40.62
50 and over	1.91	14.40

* Sources: for computing rates, United States Bureau of Commerce, Bureau of the Census, 1950 Census of Population—Advanced Reports, Series PC-14, No. 5, October 31, 1952; and Federal Bureau of Investigation, *Uniform Crime Reports for the United States and its Possessions*, Vol. XXI, No. 2 (Washington: Government Printing Office, 1950).

of this negative case but are unable to demonstrate them with the data available. The denial of the hypothesis when tested on sex is weakened, however, by three facts: (1) the proportion of all female criminals sent to prison who are committed for the crime of homicide is twice as high as the proportion of all male criminals sent to prison who are committed for the crime of homicide. (2) Since a disproportionate number of homicides are committed by Negroes, and since the status position of the Negro female equals and perhaps is higher than the status position of the Negro male, the finding that males commit more homicide than females becomes less damaging to our hypothesis. (3) The American culture pattern denies external expression of aggression to females while sanctioning it for males. Aggressive behavior is defined as a masculine trait. Docility and passivity are the prescribed feminine characteristics.[15]

Let us delay our interpretation of the negative relation between homicide and age until we have examined two additional sociological correlates of homicide, urbanism and urban ecological distributions.

Crime rates in general are positively associated with urbanism,[16] and it is often assumed that homicide is similarly related. Conclusive evidence is lacking, but several studies have been made.

Frankel comments that his findings, in New Jersey, do not confirm the higher urban homicide rates which are generally assumed to exist. By dividing New Jersey counties according to degree of urbanization, he provides us with an interesting rural-urban comparison (Table 6).

Table 6—Degree of Urbanization and Homicide in New Jersey, 1925-34*

Degree of Urbanization	Average Annual Rate of Homicide per 100,000 Population, 1925-34	Average Annual Rate of Commitment for Homicide per 100,000 population, 1925-34
Densely Urban Counties	4.29	2.69
Urban Counties	5.13	3.43
Semi-Rural Counties	4.41	3.35
Rural Counties	4.70	4.08
Total	4.49	3.00

* Source: Emil Frankel, "One Thousand Murderers," *Journal of Criminal Law and Criminology*, XXIX (January-February, 1939), pp. 672-88.

These data indicate a negative, rather than a positive, association between urbanism and homicide. "Densely Urban Counties" have the lowest average annual rate of homicide per 100,000 population and the lowest rate of commitment for homicide for the period examined. "Urban Counties" have the highest homicide rate, but "Rural Counties" have the highest rate of commitment for this offense. The greater differential between homicide rate and rate of commitment for homicide which is found in urban counties may be due to a higher proportion of murders committed by professional or organized crime. Such murders more often go unsolved than do murders committed by "legitimate" persons.

Vold quotes F.B.I. data indicating that the percentage of all rural crime comprising offenses against the person is higher than the percentage of all urban crime consisting of these types of offenses.[17] He cites Minnesota data, for which he claims greater reliability than

F.B.I. data, indicating equal rates per 100,000 population of murder and non-negligent manslaughter for both rural and urban populations of Minnesota.[18] Vold concurs with Sorokin and Zimmerman that the data "seem to indicate a tendency to higher rural rates in offenses against the person, such as homicides, infanticides, and grave assaults."[19]

We had interpreted the relation between suicide and urbanism in Chapter V as a function of differences in the degree of familial and community control over behavior in urban and rural areas. This led us to relate theoretically the positive association between suicide and urbanism and the association between suicide and marital status under the more general relationship between suicide and the strength of the relational system.

It is unfortunate that data on homicide by marital status are so limited in view of the interesting reversal in the relation of urbanism to suicide and homicide. The positive associaton between urbanism and suicide was interpreted as one of three demonstrations of the negative relation between suicide and strength of the relational system. The negative association between urbanism and homicide suggests, by the same logic, the existence of a positive relation between homicide and strength of the relational system.

This suggestion is strengthened by the decrease in homicide with age. In Chapter V we formulated the hypothesis that the strength of the relational system decreases with age to account tentatively for the positive association between suicide and age. Once again, the relation of age with suicide and homicide is reversed. Suicide varies positively and homicide varies inversely with age.

If our hypothesis that the strength of the relational system decreases with age proves to be correct, it follows that the inverse relation between homicide and age may be viewed as a second instance[20] of the positive association between homicide and strength of the relational system. If involvement in meaningful relationships with other persons proves to be at a maximum in the age groupings under 45 years and at a minimum in the categories beyond age 65, both postulates of a positive relation of homicide with strength of the relational system and a negative relation of suicide with strength of the relational system would receive strong confirmation.

If the negative relationship of homicide, and the positive relationship of suicide with urbanism reflect the positive association of homicide and the negative association of suicide with the strength of the relational system, we would predict that homicide would be lowest in the same central disorganized areas of cities where suicide is at its highest. Research forces us to reject this hypothesis. Instead of being low, homicide is in fact concentrated in these areas characterized by extremes of "urbanism." Let us summarize briefly the data on the ecological distribution of homicide.

The ecology of homicide has been investigated by Schmid and others, and has been found to follow the pattern typical of many other indices of social and personal disorganization. Schmid summarizes his findings as follows:

"First, about 25 per cent of the homicides were concentrated in a district less than ten blocks long and four blocks wide; with a population of 6,863 people, of whom less than 20 per cent are females, precincts Nos. 214, 215, 216, and 217, which constitute the large part of this district and 40 homicidal crimes, or relative to 100,000 of population, 58.0. Secondly, there is a fairly large percentage, about 20 in number, in the business district. Thirdly, computing the homicide rate of the residential sections north of Lake Union and the Lake Washington Canal with a population of 81,000 people, of whom over 50 per cent are females, and 12 homicidal deaths during decennium, 1914 to 1923 inclusive, we have the very low figure of 1.5 per 100,000 of population. Fourthly, in the industrial and residential sections in the southern part of Seattle there are about 52 homicides, which may well be considered disproportionate."[21]

More recently, Harlan has found the distribution of homicides in Birmingham to follow a similar pattern,[22] as has Lottier for the Detroit region.[23]

In spite of the general negative correlation between homicide and urbanism, more homicides are committed in the disorganized sectors of cities characterized by high residential mobility, anonymity, and extremes of "urbanism" than in the better integrated residential sections of cities. This contradiction was not present in our analysis of suicide. Studies of suicide indicated that suicide was rare in rural areas and reached its height in the central disorganized sections of cities.

The available data permit no more than the most speculative attempts to resolve this contradiction. Our other data suggested that the homicide rate would be low among presons freed from the restraints of neighborhood, family and community.

This contradiction points up sharply the difficulties in the use of ecological correlation. While the "central disorganized sectors of cities" include within them areas of "homeless men" and rooming house districts, they also include ethnic colonies composed of the more recent immigrants, Negro districts and the locus of operations of the underworld. And it is clearly impossible to determine from which one of these component sections is derived the population which accounts for the spatial correlates of suicide and homicide.

From the general negative correlation between homicide and status position, we would expect the low status ethnic and Negro inhabitants of these areas to raise the homicide rate. From the suggested relation between homicide and strength of the relational system, we would expect the "homeless men" and "anonymous" residents of rooming houses in these areas to lower the homicide rate.

Data are not presently available to permit untangling of the interrelationships among these variables in the central disorganized sectors of cities. But our formulation would lead to the suggestion that those groupings accounting for the high suicide rate in "central disorganized" areas would be sharply differentiated from those categories accounting for the high homicide rate in these same areas.

While we arc unable to separate the effects of status and strength of relational system in these areas as they effect the rate of suicide and homicide, we are able to suggest tentatively that the operation of "organized crime" within these sectors would constitute an additional factor operating to raise the homicide rate. The volume of homicide generated by organized crime is difficult to measure and undoubtedly fluctuates with the intensity of gang warfare. Numerous writers have pointed out the rigidity and integration of the underworld culture. With its own set of values, techniques and tight social organization, the underworld society maintains exceedingly strong control over its members as a condition for survival in opposition to the legitimate world of law and order.[24]

Furthermore, one of the tools of the underworld is homicide. Murder of the stool pigeon is evidence of the seriousness with which violation of the social code is taken. The underworld culture sanctions and encourages the use of violence against legitimate society.

Data are not available indicating the extent to which murders as part of the routine business of the underworld account for the high rates of homicide in disorganized areas. We suggest the hypothesis, however, that the high homicide rate may be accounted for in part by the maneuvers of organized crime, a highly integrated community operating within the anonymity of these disorganized areas.

The violent and murderous tendencies in the underworld culture, viewed in terms of our general theoretical formulation, provide support for the hypothesis that the external expression of aggression varies positively with the strength of external restraint. The underworld, viewed as a system, is subjected to constant pressure and restraint by legitimate society. The fact that the strong external restraints are associated with crimes of violence by the group subjected to the restraint provides a test of the hypothesis when applied at the system level.

▶ INTERPRETATION

Our examination of the relation between homicide and social control has been hampered by lack of data in many crucial areas. But using the research available, we have tried to test two hypotheses suggested by the material on suicide presented in Chapter V. Neither of these hypotheses has been tested adequately, but in both cases, the available data tend to confirm rather than to deny them.

The first hypothesis states a negative relation between status and homicide. The hypothesis held up when tested on race and by region, comparing rates in the industrial North and the economically depressed South, with race held constant. The homicide rate among Negroes, the low status category, is some ten times as high as the homicide rate among white persons, the higher status category.

Data by sex and age deny the hypothesis. Since males commit more of all crimes than females, and since cultural definitions about external expression of aggression differ radically by sex, the finding that females commit more homicide relative to other types of crime than males weakens this negative case. The positive association between status by sex and homicide is further weakened by the fact that the status differential between Negro males and females (the race committing a disproportionate number of homicides) is slight. In fact certain writers suggest that the status of the lower class Negro female may be higher than that of the Negro male. As in the case of suicide, the relation with status by age contradicts the hypothesis.

The second hypothesis states a positive relation between homicide and the degree of involvement in social or cathectic relationships with other persons. If this hypothesis is correct, the homicide rate among the married should exceed the rate among the single, the widowed or the divorced. Durkheim's data do in fact indicate that "while family life has a moderating effect upon suicide, it rather stimulates murder."[25] Adequate test of this hypothesis for the United States would provide an important link in the test of our formulation. The available data, unfortunately, group together the sizable widowed and divorced categories and fail to discriminate between those who become "single," widowed or even "divorced" by murdering the spouse and those who belong to these categories because they either have never married or were legitimately widowed or divorced. If adequate test in the United States should confirm Durkheim's finding, it would provide striking support for the proposition that suicide varies negatively and homicide positively with the strength of the relational system.

The higher homicide rates found in rural as compared with urban areas support this proposition. In areas of extreme urbanism—the disorganized central sectors of large cities—the homicide rate is relatively high whereas the hypothesis predicts that it would be relatively low. Further, this finding is inconsistent with data showing a general negative association between homicide and urbanism. Evidence is inadequate to assess the relative importance of the presence in disorganized areas of low status ethnic and Negro categories which might be expected to have high rates of homicide. The presence of organized crime in these areas may account in part for the high rate of homicide since (a) murder is an approved tool of gang warfare and (b) aggressive behavior in response to the external restraints imposed on the underworld by legitimate society would be predicted by our formulation.

Homicide was found to be concentrated in the younger age categories. This is the reverse of the relation between age and suicide, with the highest rates of suicide centered in the older age groupings. In Chapter V we had suggested the hypothesis that the strength of the relational system decreases with increasing age. It is worthy of note that if further research should confirm this hypothesis, it would at the same time support our postulation of a negative association between suicide and strength of the relational system and of a positive association between homicide and strength of the relational system.

The data of this Chapter provide a very tentative confirmation of our two hypotheses, that homicide varies negatively with status and positively with strength of the relational system. The variables of status and degree of involvement in meaningful relationships have been related conceptually to the strength of external restraints over behavior.

Low status persons are required to conform to the demands and expectations of others by virtue of their low status. We have labeled the type of external restraint varying with status position as "vertical" restraint over behavior or restraint imposed by persons or groups higher in the status system. The strength of vertical external restraint decreases with increasing status. Our data showing a negative relation between homicide and status position lead us to the postulate that homicide varies positively with the strength of vertical external restraint.

Persons with strong relational systems are required to conform to the demands and expectations of others as a condition of the maintenance of these relationships. Persons involved in minimal relationships with other persons are subject to fewer demands and expectations simply by virtue of the slight degree of involvement. We have labeled the type of external restraint varying with the strength of the relational system as "horizontal" restraint over behavior, or restraint imposed by other parties to the relationship. The strength of horizontal external restraint increases as the strength of the relational system increases.

Our data very tentatively indicating a positive association between homicide and strength of the relational system lead us to the postulate that homicide varies positively with the strength of horizontal external restraint. Test of the hypotheses (1) that homicide rates are higher for the married than for the non-married, and (2) that the strength of the relational system decreases with age will provide either effective confirmation or effective denial of this postulate.

Our two postulates, empirically derived from gross sociological correlates of homicide, both state a positive relation between homicide and the strength of external restraint over behavior. In Chapter V, two postulates, empirically derived from the gross sociological correlates of suicide, both state a negative relation between suicide and the strength of external restraint over behavior.

These postulates may be summarized in the tentative proposition that suicide varies negatively and homicide positively with the strength of external restraint over behavior. An attempt is made in Part III to relate this proposition to the frustration-aggression hypothesis, as tested on the relationships of suicide and homicide with the business cycle, and to the clinical formulations of suicide and homicide.

part three

SOME PSYCHOLOGICAL

DETERMINANTS OF THE CHOICE

BETWEEN SUICIDE AND HOMICIDE

chapter VII

BASES FOR THE LEGITIMIZATION

OF OTHER-ORIENTED

AGGRESSION

► SOCIOLOGICAL BASES

We have discussed in Part I the relation of suicide and homicide with the business cycle and have concluded that the relationships are congruent with the formulation of suicide and homicide as types of aggressive acts which respond in a consistent way to objective frustrations generated by the flow of economic forces. Suicide and homicide were treated as undifferentiated acts of aggression in the sense that they react in the same way to the same objective frustrating source.

In Part II, our two types of aggressive acts were differentiated in terms of differences in the target of the aggression. In suicide, the target of the aggression is the self. In homicide, the target of the aggression is another person. We concluded that the choice of target for the aggression was in part a function of the strength of external restraint over behavior. When behavior is required to conform rigidly to the demands and expectations of other persons, the probability of suicide as a response to frustration is low and the probability of homicide as a response to frustration is high. When behavior is freed from the requirement for conformity to the de-

101

mands and expectations of others, the probability of suicide is high and the probability of homicide is low.

Let us assume, before beginning our discussion of the bases of legitimization of the expression of aggression, that the basic and primary target of aggression is another person rather than the self. Let us further assume that the degree to which aggression consequent to frustration is "other-oriented" (directed outwardly against another person) varies positively with the degree to which other-oriented aggression is defined by the aggressor as legitimate. With these assumptions, "self-oriented" aggression consequent to frustration becomes a residual category or aggression for which outward expression against others is denied legitimacy. Homicide thus would occur as a response to frustration only when the other-oriented expression of aggression was defined by the aggressor as highly legitimate.

If it is true that war lowers the suicide rate and raises the homicide rate, holding constant the effect of business conditions, the explanation may lie in the fact that war not only legitimizes but acts to encourage the expression of aggression outwardly against the enemy. Frustration suffered during times of war can always be blamed on the enemy. The focusing of aggression against the opponent fulfills an important social function.

By placing homicide at one extreme of a continuum of legitimacy of other-oriented aggression and by placing suicide at the other extreme, we are able to restate our empirical proposition that suicide varies negatively and homicide positively with the strength of external restraint over behavior. If our two assumptions are correct, the degree of legitimization of other-oriented aggression consequent to frustration varies positively with the strength of external restraint over behavior.

The strength of external restraint thus becomes our primary basis for the legitimization of other-oriented aggression. When behavior is required to conform rigidly to the demands and expectations of others (when external restraints are strong) our proposition would suggest that the expression of aggression against others is legitimized. When behavior is freed from the requirement of conformity to the demands and expectations of others (when external restraints are weak), the expression of aggression against others fails to be legitimized.

As the degree to which behavior is determined by the demands and expectations of others increases, the share of others in responsibility for the consequences of the behavior also increases. If a person commits an act primarily because others want him to commit it, others must share responsibility for the consequences of the act. If the act is committed independently of the demands and expectations of other persons, other persons cannot very well be held responsible if the consequences are unfortunate.

As the role of others in the determination of behavior increases, the right to blame others for unfortunate consequences also increases. When the role of the self in determining behavior is great relative to the role of others, the self must bear responsibility for the consequences of the behavior.

When behavior is subjected to strong external restraints by virtue either of subordinate status or intense involvement in social relationships with other persons, the restraining objects can be blamed for frustration, thereby legitimizing outward expression of the resultant aggression. When behavior is freed from external restraint, the self must bear the responsibility for frustration. Others cannot be blamed since others were not involved in the determination of behavior. Under these conditions, other-oriented expression of the resultant aggression fails to be legitimized.

The strength of external restraint—our sociological basis of legitimization of other oriented aggression—was derived from our study of the structural correlates of suicide and homicide in adult life.

▶ PSYCHOLOGICAL BASES FOR THE LEGITIMIZATION
   OF OTHER-ORIENTED AGGRESSION

Psychoanalytic writers have been most concerned with the first "psychological" basis of legitimization of other-oriented aggression consequent to frustration—the intensity of super-ego formation or guilt in the child. The super-ego—the system of demands and expectations imposed on the child by the parents *as internalized* by the child—operates in part to control the expression of "instinctual" forces, including the expression of aggression outwardly against others. This in no sense minimizes either the existence or importance of other functional components of the super-ego. Freud's classic statement reads as follows:

"Its relation to the ego is not exhausted by the precept: 'You *ought to be* such and such (like your father)'; it also comprises the prohibition: 'You *must not be* such and such (like your father); that is, you may not do all that he does; many things are his prerogative.' "[1]

These functions, contradictory at first glance, are perfectly consistent if we define the super-ego as consisting of the system of demands and expectations imposed on the child by the parents as internalized by the child. This system of demands and expectations then becomes the system of demands and expectations imposed on the child by himself.

In the psychoanalytic formulation of suicide, for example, the strict and punitive demands of parents become internalized in the form of a strict and punitive super-ego which operates to turn aggression against the self. It was perhaps this aspect of suicide which led Durkheim to the "altruistic" type, attributed to "insufficient individuation" of the person.

Five different studies suggest that a weak or defective super-ego formation is associated with other-oriented aggression while a strict super-ego formation is associated with self-oriented aggression.

Reiss, in an empirical study of the "personal controls" of delinquents, found that delinquents with "defective super-ego controls" had higher rates of delinquent recidivism than delinquents with "relatively integrated personal controls."[2] [3] Clearly, this study would provide better evidence if we knew the relation between super-ego strength and types of specifically aggressive delinquency.

Aichhorn does suggest such an association between inadequate super-ego formation and "aggressive" delinquency.

"We shall have accounted for many expressions of delinquency when we recognize that either the ego-ideal (used synonomously with super-ego) may lack some of the qualities which society demands or that the ego-ideal may take up socially acceptable demands in a distorted way or not at all."[4]

In her discussion of "identification with the aggressor," Anna

Freud notes a similar relation between inadequate "internalization of the critical process" and the outward expression of aggression.

"In 'identification with the aggressor' we recognize a by no means uncommon stage in the normal development of the super-ego. When the . . . cases I have just described identified themselves with their elders' threats of punishment, they were taking an important step towards the formation of that institution: they were internalizing other people's criticisms of their behavior. When a child constantly repeats this process of internalization and introjects the qualities of those responsible for his upbringing, making their characteristics and opinions his own, he is all the time providing material from which the super-ego may take shape. But at this point children are not quite wholehearted in acknowledging that institution. The internalized criticism is not as yet immediately transformed into self-criticism. As we have seen . . . it is dissociated from the child's own reprehensible activity and turned back on the outside world. By means of a new defensive process identification with the aggressor is succeeded by an active assault on the outside world."[5]

Further,

"it is possible that a number of people remain arrested at the intermediate stage in the development of the super-ego and never quite complete the internalization of the critical process."[6]

With the assumption that super-ego strength is greater among persons who refuse to cheat than among cheaters, a study by MacKinnon yields further evidence on the relation between direction of expression of aggression and super-ego strength. He found that cheaters tend to express aggression outwardly while non-cheaters tend to express aggression against themselves. The non-cheaters also said they had experienced more guilt feelings in the past than did the cheaters.[7]

Finally, Heinicke presents evidence to show that young boys with high guilt tend to express less overt or outward aggression than boys with low guilt.[8]

All five of these studies tend to support the view found frequently in the clinical literature that weak or inadequate super-ego formation is associated with inadequate control of aggressive impulses while strict super-ego formation is associated with the inhibition of "other-oriented" aggression. And the writers cited in Appendix I are in agreement that the strong punitive super-ego is associated with suicide—the expression of aggression against the self.

A second psychological basis of legitimization of other-oriented aggression is found in the psycho-physiological literature. King studied the relationship between the direction of expression of aggression and cardiovascular reaction during experimentally-induced stress.[9] He found that the response of anger directed outwardly against others was associated with a specific type of cardiovascular reaction termed "nor-epinephrine-like" because it was similar to that produced by an injection of nor-epinephrine. Subjects responding with anger directed against the self, or with anxiety experienced a different type of cardiovascular reaction which they termed "epinephrine-like" because of its similarity to that produced by an injection of epinephrine. The association between the response of "other-oriented" aggression and a nor-epinephrine-like cardiovascular reaction was significant beyond the .001 level.

These two psychological correlates of the direction of expression of aggression—super-ego strength and cardiovascular reaction during stress—are related in the following section to aspects of the parent-child relationship with the hope that an understanding of their early childhood correlates may help in further reducing the unexplained variance in rates of suicide and homicide.

▶ PARENT-CHILD CORRELATES OF TWO PSYCHOLOGICAL BASES OF
   LEGITIMIZATION OF OTHER-ORIENTED AGGRESSION

Super-ego Strength.—The clinical literature yields somewhat contradictory statements on the relation between super-ego strength and the degree of control imposed upon children by their parents. Anna Freud's formulation of "identification with the aggressor" seems to imply that those who never "quite complete the internalization of the critical process" and identify with the aggressor are the offspring of strict, critical and aggressive parents. Aichhorn, in his clinical study of aggressive behavior and delinquency found that this type of delinquency—associated with defective super-ego formation— arises most frequently from an "excess of severity."[10]

A recent study by Heinicke supports the view that parental severity is associated with a weak and inadequate super-ego formation. He defined the two end points of a continuum of internalization of parental values as fear and guilt and found that young boys at the "fear" end of the continuum (with inadequate super-ego formation) received more punishment and less nurturance than those falling at the "guilt" end.

". . . it seems that the children in the *F* (Fear) group were in general punished more and their mothers tended to use such techniques as physical punishment rather than control by reasoning."[11]

In contrast with these studies which may be interpreted as suggesting that parental severity is associated with weak or inadequate internalization of the "critical process," are the writings on the relation of super-ego formation and the resolution of the Oedipus complex. Freud writes:

"The authority of the father or the parents is introjected into the ego, and there forms the kernel of the super-ego, which takes its severity from the father, perpetuates his prohibition against incest, and so insures the ego against a recurrence of the libidinal object cathexes."[12]

This statement suggests that the greater the severity of the father towards the son, the greater will be the severity of the super-ego in its domination over the ego. This is further clarified in the following quotation.

"The super-ego retains the character of the father, while the more intense the Oedipus complex was and the more rapidly it succumbed to repression (under the influence of discipline, religious teaching, schooling and reading) the more exacting later on is the domination of the super-ego over the ego—in the form of conscience or perhaps of an unconscious sense of guilt."[13]

While these statements suggest that paternal severity is associated with strict and punitive super-ego formation, they further suggest a relation between super-ego formation and abandonment of the "libidinal object cathexes." A quotation from Fenichel illustrates this aspect of the psychoanalytic formulation of super-ego development.

"An important step in further maturation is accomplished when prohibitions set up by parents remain effective even in their absence. Now a constant watchman has been instituted in the mind, who signals the approach of possible situations or behavior that might result in the loss of the mother's affection, or the approach of an occasion to earn the reward of the mother's affection . . . a portion of the ego has become an "inner mother," threatening a possible withdrawal of affection."[14]

Two empirical studies strongly buttress the implied hypothesis that withdrawal of love operates to increase internalization and super-ego strength.

Whiting and Child[15] in their cross-cultural studies found that a frequent use of "love-oriented" techniques of punishment was associated with a high degree of guilt. The degree of internalization was measured by rating the extent to which people in a society assumed responsibility for sickness. They argued that people who blame themselves for sickness are showing more of a guilt reaction than those who put the blame for illness on others. They found that the techniques of denial of love, threats of denial of reward and threats of ostracism were more often found in high guilt cultures while the technique of physical punishment was more often found in low guilt cultures. Heinicke, in a study of 4 and 5 year old American boys, was able to confirm the results of the cross-cultural study. He found that mothers of "high guilt" boys more frequently used love-oriented techniques of punishment—denial of love and deprivation—while mothers of "low guilt" boys more frequently used "spanking" or other forms of physical punishment.[16]

Before proceeding to the parent-child correlates of cardiovascular reaction during stress, an additional finding of Heinicke should be noted. His three guilt groups—boys with high, medium and low guilt—did not differ in the amounts of nurturance they received from the parents. This enabled him to compare the relative roles of mother and father in discipline and control of the child holding constant the effects of nurturance. He found that for the high guilt group, the mother was the primary source of discipline and control over the child. For the low guilt group, the father played a relatively greater role in controlling the child. The relative amounts of authority, strictness, discipline and demands for obedience imposed by the mother were greater among the high guilt than among the low guilt groups.[17]

Let us now summarize the parent-child correlates of guilt and super-ego strength.

1. Theoretical writings on the relation between parental severity and super-ego strength appear contradictory. Some suggest that a

weak or defective super-ego is associated with parental severity. Others suggest that a strict and punitive super-ego is associated with parental severity. Both the empirical studies of Aichhorn and Heinicke support the view that extreme parental severity is associated with weak or inadequate super-ego formation.

2. The theoretical writings of Freud, the cross-cultural studies of Whiting and Child and Heinicke's work all point to the role of loss of love in internalization or super-ego formation. The two empirical studies present convincing evidence that the withholding or withdrawal of love is associated with a high degree of internalization and guilt.

3. Heinicke found that the mothers of high guilt boys were the primary source of frustration and discipline as compared with the fathers. Fathers of low guilt boys played a relatively greater role in discipline.

Cardiovascular reaction during stress.—King and Henry[18] found that the type of cardiovascular reaction experienced by male college students during experimentally-induced stress was associated with the degree of severity of discipline by the father and the relative roles of mother and father in the administration of discipline. Data on paternal severity and the relative roles of each parent in discipline were derived from questionnaires administered to the sons who were the subjects in the experiment.

Their measures of severity of the father are highly correlated with their measures of dominance of the father relative to the mother in discipline. Subjects who reported the father as strict also reported the father was the principle disciplinarian in the family. Those who reported the father as mild in discipline reported that the mother was the principal disciplinarian.

The association between severity of the father and a nor-epinephrine-like cardiovascular reaction during stress was significant at the .06 level. The association between dominance of the father and nor-epinephrine-like cardiovascular reaction was significant beyond the .01 level.

There were 11 subjects (about 10 per cent of the sample) who reported (a) that their mothers were strict (b) that their fathers were not strict and (c) that the mother was the principal disciplinarian in the family. Only one of these 11 subjects had a nor-epinephrine-like cardiovascular reaction during stress. This is in sharp contrast to the nearly 100 per cent nor-epinephrine-like reactions of subjects reporting strict fathers, lenient mothers and the father as the principal disciplinarian. Severity and dominance of the father relative to the mother was associated with a nor-epinephrine-like pattern. Severity and dominance of the mother relative to the father was associated with an epinephrine-like pattern.

Interpretation.—We have examined the parent-child correlates of our two "psychological" bases of legitimization of other-oriented aggression—super-ego strength or guilt and cardiovascular reaction during stress.

The super-ego correlates lead us tentatively to two conclusions. (1) "Love-oriented" techniques of discipline are associated with strong super-ego formation and high guilt while techniques of punishment not threatening loss of love are associated with inadequate super-ego formation and low guilt. (2) The relative disciplinary roles of mother and father are associated with super-ego formation and guilt. When the mother rather than the father plays the dominant disciplinary role in the family, the male child tends to develop a strict super-ego and high guilt.

The cardiovascular correlates lead us tentatively to the conclusion that severity and dominance of the mother relative to the father in disciplining the male child is associated with an epinephrine-like cardiovascular reaction.

It is important to note that when the mother rather than the father is the primary source of discipline and control, the consequences are manifested both in a strong super-ego with high guilt (Heinicke) and an epinephrine-like cardiovascular reaction during stress (King and Henry). This is of particular relevance in view of the fact that both of the consequences are associated with self-oriented aggression and suggest the hypothesis that persons reacting with an epinephrine-like cardiovascular pattern during stress would be defined clinically as "guilt-ridden" and possessing a strict super-ego.

The evidence that love-oriented techniques of discipline are associated with the development of high guilt is compelling. Let us utilize that fact, together with the relation between maternal dominance and guilt in an attempt to resolve the apparent contradictions in the clinical formulations of the relation between parental severity and guilt. Certain of the theoretical formulations of super-ego development predict that a strict and punitive super-ego derives from identification with strict and punitive parents while certain empirical studies advance the contrasting view that parental severity is associated with weak inadequate super-ego development. We will suggest that both of these apparently contradictory relationships do exist in fact and that the contradiction disappears when the role of denial of love in the socialization process is introduced.

Let us assume that initially, all aggressive responses consequent to frustration are directed outwardly against the external source of the frustration. Let us also assume that the degree of severity of control imposed on the child by the parents indexes the degree of frustration to which the child is subjected.

With these assumptions, together with the frustration-aggression hypothesis which we have assumed throughout this study, it follows that the quantity of the aggression expressed outwardly by the infant (prior to internalization) will vary directly with the severity of control imposed by the parents. It is necessary to further define this relationship with respect to each parent as follows. (1) The quantity of aggression expressed outwardly by the infant against the mother will vary directly with the severity of control imposed by the mother. (2) The quantity of aggression expressed outwardly by the infant against the father will vary directly with the severity of control imposed by the father.

We have been deliberate in failing to specify the type of control imposed since the evidence already cited indicates that type of control is relevant for the process of internalization and ultimately for the direction of expression of aggression. But it is not relevant for the quantity of aggression which is a consequence of frustration and which we have assumed varies with the severity of control. We have been cautious in maintaining throughout that the degree of frustration is relevant for the degree of consequent aggression but is not relevant in the determination of the direction in which the subsequent aggression will be expressed.

Heinicke found that subjects with "fear" or inadequate super-ego formation received more punishment and less nurturance than subjects with "guilt" or strong super-ego formation. And it is likely that these two variables are inversely correlated. If so, in cases of extreme parental severity, the child receives very little affection. If there is very little affection or love for the child, there is very little opportunity for the effective use of "love-oriented" techniques of punishment. In the absence of techniques of withdrawal of love, the child subjected to severe punishment would fail to internalize parental values and be characterized as having inadequate super-ego formation. This formulation is also congruent with the findings of Aichhorn that the child subjected to an "excess of severity" fails to internalize parental criticism.

But with sufficient love and nurturance, one would expect the child to develop love for the nurturant parent just as we would expect the child to develop aggression against the frustrating parent. Parsons has noted this relationship.

"That cathexis of a human object . . . is highly contingent on the responsiveness of the object is a fact familiar to psychoanalytic theory. It may be regarded as almost a truism that it is difficult if not impossible in the long run to love without being loved in return."[19]

Parents, viewed both as the source of nurturance and the source of frustration, provide a basis in their children both for love and hate of the parents—the love consequent to the nurturance and the hate consequent to the frustration.

In beginning our discussion of the relative roles played by mother and father in nurturance and frustration of the child, let us assume that, at least for the male child, the mother represents the principal source of nurturance and love. If the mother is also the principal source of frustration, the source of nurturance and the source of frustration is centered in the same parental role. When the mother is the principal source of frustration, aggression of the child consequent to the frustration will be directed against the mother, as the source of frustration. Our empirical evidence suggests that when the mother rather than the father is the principal source of frustration, the consequences for the child are manifested both in a strong super-ego (high guilt) and an epinephrine-like cardiovascular pattern during stress. Both of these consequences are associated with a tendency to express aggression inwardly against the self. We also know, from the cross-cultural work, that high guilt is associated with the use of "withdrawal of love" as a technique of discipline. And from the evidence previously cited on the association between guilt and self-oriented aggression, we may assume that a tendency to express aggression against the self is associated with the use of "withdrawal of love" as a technique of punishment. This assumption is given additional support in view of the way in which guilt was defined in the Whiting-Child study as the tendency for the self to assume responsibility for illness. Some clinicians would assert that blaming the self for illness is a form of expression of aggression against the self.

These studies suggest a tentative interpretation of the fact that maternal dominance is associated with high guilt and an epinephrine-like cardiovascular reaction during stress. If we are correct in suggesting that the dominant mother is on the one hand the target of infantile aggression and on the other the source of the infant's love, the aggression may threaten or cut off the flow of nurturance. If further research should show that the use of love-oriented techniques of punisment is high when the source of love is the same as the target of aggression, it would provide evidence for the hypothesis that the degree of internalization varies with the degree to which aggression threatens nurturance. When the mother is dominant, the target of aggression is the same as the source of nurturance. When the target of aggression is the source of nurturance, the aggression is more likely to threaten nurturance. The more the aggression threatens nurturance, the greater will be the inhibition of the aggression.

If aggression against the mother is inhibited because it threatens the flow of nurturance, we would also expect the maximum internalization of maternal values to occur when aggression threatens the mother's love. If aggression threatens nurturance, then behavior of the child which fails to conform to the maternal demands and expectations would also be likely to threaten nurturance. The outward expression of aggression against the mother must be inhibited as a means of avoiding the loss of the mother's love. And at the same time, the demands and expectations of the mother towards the son are internalized as a means of guarding against further action which will again jeopardize the flow of nurturance; ". . . a portion of the ego has become an 'inner mother,' threatening a possible withdrawal of affection."[20]

This very tentative attempt to bring certain of the parent-child

correlates of our two psychological bases of legitimization of other-
oriented aggression to bear on our problem must await further
research for confirmation or rejection. But before we examine
certain of the implications for suicide and homicide, let us return
to the apparent "contradiction" found in certain of the theoretical
formulations of super-ego strength. Some suggest that a weak or
defective super-ego is associated with parental severity while others
suggest that a strict and punitive super-ego is associated with
parental severity.

We have assumed that initially all aggressive responses consequent to frustration are directed outwardly against the source of
frustration and that the degree of severity imposed on the child by
the parents indexes the degree of frustration to which the child is
subjected. Therefore, the greater the severity of the parents, the
greater the aggression of the child against the parents.

Now let us assume a high level of parental severity and a high
amount of consequent childhood aggression. And let us vary the
degree to which the aggression threatens nurturance. Our formulation would suggest that when the aggression jeopardizes nurturance,
it will be inhibited, and aggression aroused by subsequent frustration will be expressed inwardly against the self rather than outwardly against the source of frustration. The concomitant high
level of internalization of the severe and punitive parental attitude
would produce a severe and punitive super-ego in the child. The
severe and punitive attitude of the parent towards the child would
become, after internalization, a severe and critical attitude of the
child towards himself.

Now let us assume that the aggression generated by severe parents does not jeopardize the flow of love to the child. Since nurturance is not threatened by the aggression, internalization of parental attitudes will be minimal and inhibition or "turning inward"
of the aggression does not take place. The aggression will continue
to be expressed outwardly against the source of frustration and the
super-ego development will be weak and defective.

We have suggested that the degree to which aggression threatens nurturance and love may vary with the distributions of the
functions of nurturance and discipline between the two parental

roles and have assumed that the mother is the principal source of nurturance. Aichhorn notes the case where delinquency arises from a very severe father coupled with an indulgent mother who sides with the child in rebellion against the father. Since nurturance is in no sense threatened by the aggression, the aggression continues and inhibition and internalization of parental values fails to take place. But when the aggression generated by parental severity threatens the flow of maternal nurturance, the studies available support the hypothesis that a strict and punitive super-ego derives from severe parental control.

▶ IMPLICATIONS FOR SUICIDE AND HOMICIDE

We have examined our two psychological bases of legitimization of other-oriented aggression—super-ego strength and cardiovascular reaction during stress—and have concluded that the "psychological" legitimization of other-oriented aggression consequent to frustration varies inversely with the degree to which other-oriented aggression threatens or has threatened the flow of nurturance and love. Let us now see whether this conclusion will help in explaining certain differences in rates of suicide which cannot be accounted for in terms of the degree of external restraint over behavior.

The reader will recall that suicide rates of the married within each age category are lower than rates of the single, the widowed or the divorced in the same age categories. This fact was interpreted as a function of differences in the degree of external restraint operative for the married as compared with the single, widowed and divorced. The behavior of the married person, immersed in a stronger relational system, is required to conform more to the demands and expectations of others than is the behavior of the single, widowed or divorced person.

While our "sociological" basis of legitimization of other-oriented aggression—the strength of external restraint—can account for the lower suicide rate among the married, it cannot account for differences between the three "weak restraint" categories. Since the case of the single category is complicated by the fact that there are no children, let us look at the differences in the suicide rates of the widowed and the divorced holding constant the effects of age and sex. Both categories are similar in the sense that members of both have been married and the members of both have lost the spouse. But in the case of the divorced, the loss of the spouse was a function of a deliberate and motivated act while in the case of the widowed the loss of the spouse occurred through death—a loss independent of the wishes of the surviving partner.

If we make the assumptions (1) that the act of divorce is evidence of the expression of aggression against the spouse and (2) that prior to the divorce the spouse was a primary source of nurturance and love, we are able to suggest that for the divorced, the consequence of aggression was the loss of nurturance. For the widowed the loss of love was a consequence of death independent of aggression against the spouse.

With these assumptions, we would predict from our "psychological" basis of legitimization of other-oriented aggression that the divorced would have higher suicide rates than the widowed of the same age and sex. The data conform with this prediction. In certain age categories, the suicide rate among the divorced is twice as high as the suicide rate among the widowed of the same sex. And in all age categories past 25, the suicide rate of the divorced is greater than the suicide rate of the widowed.[21]

We suggest that loss of love as a function of aggression directed against the source of nurturance may have an effect for the divorced similar to that which produces guilt and the inhibition of aggression in the child when his aggression threatens the flow of nurturance. Aggression against the marital partner destroys the marriage and with it a primary source of nurturance and love. The resultant inhibition of aggression and internalization of the attitudes of the source of frustration serve to deny legitimacy to outward expression of aggression consequent to future frustration and the result is an increased tendency to express aggression inwardly against the self.

The psychological basis of legitimization of other-oriented aggression may also be helpful in accounting for the empirical fact that suicide and homicide often are committed by the same person. In England and Wales in 1949, 100 persons over one year of age

were murdered. And in 34 of these cases, the murderer or sus-
pected murderer committed suicide.[22] Even if this ratio is biased
in favor of the law enforcement authorities, it indicates a remarkable correspondence between the two types of aggressive act.

If the foregoing analysis is correct, it would suggest that those
who follow homicide with suicide can be differentiated from those
who do not follow homicide with suicide in terms of the degree
to which the act of murder destroys a primary source of nurturance
and love. If the aggression operates to destroy the flow of nurturance, we would expect—as in the case of divorce—a resultant inhibition of aggression and internalization of the values of the source
of frustration. These processes would serve to deny legitimacy to
outward expression of aggression consequent to future frustration
and the result would be an increased tendency to express aggression inwardly against the self. Murder destroys the source of frustration in the external world. The internalization consequent to the
loss of nurturance re-establishes the source of frustration within
the self. And the self becomes the legitimate target for aggression.

It is likely that those who commit suicide after divorce and those
who commit suicide after murder are persons with strong super-
ego formation who have internalized prohibitions against the outward expression of aggression consequent to the events of childhood with which we have been concerned. But if this is true, we
are faced with a contradiction. For we have shown that these
persons with high guilt tend to express aggression inwardly against
themselves rather than outwardly against others. How can we account for the fact that these persons commit murder in the first
place?

Clinical reports of the frequency of *projection* in cases of homicide may help us in the resolution of this dilemma.

Patterson's "Psychiatric Study of Juveniles Involved in Homicide"
found that one of the "outstanding characteristics of the group as
a whole was the incidence of mother attachment and father ha-
tred."[23] The "oedipus-electra" themes recur in the clinical literature
of homicide. Writers report that the male murderer often kills the
mother surrogate—his wife, mistress, or a female with whom he
has carried on an apparently platonic relationship.[24] Meyer and his

associates report the histories of fourteen men who murdered women. They find the oedipus situation underlies a wide variety of apparent or precipitating factors in these murders. They conclude:

"From the first to the last of these cases run similarly rationalized justifications. The women murdered were without exception regarded by their murderers as threatening agents who invited, who forced their own destruction. The themes of infidelity, sexual rejection, loss of money and status, venereal infection contracted from the woman occurred singly or in concert in each of these fourteen histories, or they were bizarrely distorted into the psychotic's conviction that he had been 'conjured' or 'hypnotized.' "[25]

These writings suggest that internalized or super-ego demands on behavior often are projected onto the victim and invested with reality in the external world. If through the mechanism of the projection of guilt,[26] the harsh discipline imposed by the super-ego is "externalized" and attributed to some real person in the external world, the projection would at the same time weaken the internalized prohibition against the outward expression of aggression and provide an effective (though imagined) source of frustration in the external world. It was W. I. Thomas who years ago pointed out that when situations are defined as real, they are real in their consequences.[26]

We started our discussion with the problem of internalization of parental demands and expectations and the associated inhibition of outward expression of aggression. And we are ending our discussion with the problem of projection—the "externalization" of these same internalized demands and expectations. Neither of these processes is adequately understood. Yet both seem highly relevant for the problem of the "psychological" basis of legitimacy of other-oriented aggression.

In bringing our study to a close, let us re-state our sociological and psychological bases of legitimacy of other-oriented aggression. Internalization of harsh parental demands and discipline produces a high "psychological probability" of suicide and a low "psychological probability" of homicide. We have suggested that the "psychological" determination of the legitimacy of other-oriented aggression is a function of the degree to which childhood aggression threatens nurturance. Clearly, this "psychological" basis cannot in and of itself explain the persistent variations in the suicide and homicide rates at differing points in the social structure and the life cycle.[27]

We have accounted tentatively for differences in rates of suicide and homicide at differing points in the social structure and the life cycle with the proposition that the legitimization of other-oriented aggression varies directly with the strength of external restraint over behavior of the adult—external restraint which is a function of strength of the relational system and position in the status hierarchy. Strong external restraints in adult life produce a high "sociological probability" of homicide consequent to frustration and a low "sociological probability" of suicide consequent to frustration.

In Part I, we have attempted to show that both suicide and homicide react in the same way to one objective source of frustration—loss of status consequent to the flow of economic forces. And in our discussion of the sociological and psychological bases of legitimacy of other-oriented aggression we have specified certain of the factors which determine whether the aggression consequent to the frustration is directed inwardly against the self or outwardly against others.

The highly tentative nature of our formulation has been pointed out many times in the course of its development. It is our hope that empirical test of the hypotheses suggested in the final Chapter will produce ever closer conceptual approximations to the reality of the problem with which we have struggled.

In the course of this volume we have used mass data in the test of hypotheses about individual behavior. The logical and methodological problems of this procedure are many, yet the advantages appear to outweigh the disadvantages. With our task of locating points of congruence between the economic, sociological and psychological aspects of suicide and homicide, it became useful to deal with mass data in order to secure as broad a base for generalization as possible.

At many points in the development of the argument, inadequacy of the available data was made explicit and suggestions for further research were offered. In this Chapter we suggest an experimental test of the proposition with which our work ends—that the degree of legitimization of other-directed aggression varies positively with the strength of external restraint over behavior. This proposition has emerged out of examination of the economic, sociological and psychological correlates of our two types of aggressive act and can be tested independently of the method by which it was derived. It predicts that strong external restraints will increase the probability of other-directed aggression by providing a basis for its legitimization.

Operational definition of "strength of external restraint" is needed. This variable is defined as the degree to which behavior is required to conform to the demands and expectations of others in the external world. It can be defined operationally as the degree of compulsion used in the selection of subjects for experimentation. If a sample were composed of students enrolled in a college course, those volunteering to take part in the experiment would be classed as those with weak external restraints. Their participation in the experiment would be of their own choosing—a choice independent of any requirement for conformity to the demands and expectations of the instructor. A second group, with strong external restraints, would be required to participate in the experiment in order to fulfill the formal course requirement. They would be allowed no choice in the matter.

Let us then expose our subjects to a constant source of frustration and measure the degree to which the aggression generated by the frustration is directed against the self. We would predict that those subjects who volunteered willingly for the experiment would react to the frustration with more self-oriented aggression than those who were participating under duress. Figure 1 illustrates the predicted response to the experimental frustration for each of four groups on the assumption that we can also measure the strength of internal restraint. When weak external restraints and strong internal restraints are operating to deny legitimacy to other-oriented aggression, we would predict a high probability of self-oriented aggression (a in Figure 1).

Figure 1

	Strong Internalized Restraints	Weak Internalized Restraints
Weak External Restraints	(a) self-oriented aggression	(c) unpredictable
Strong External Restraints	(b) anxiety or conflict	(d) other-oriented aggression

When strong external restraints are legitimizing other-oriented aggression and when internal restraints are weak, we predict a high probability of other-oriented aggression in response to frustration (d in Figure 1). The remaining two cases are more difficult to predict. If strong external restraints are acting to legitimize aggression outward and strong internal restraints are acting to prohibit outward expression of aggression, we would predict anxiety or conflict since the two bases of legitimization of other-oriented aggression are operating in opposite directions (b in Figure 1).

This case may be similar to anxiety and neurotic reactions of men returning from combat service. If the war is treated as a factor legitimizing and encouraging other-oriented aggression, the outbreak of anxiety may result from conflict created for the person with strong internalized prohibitions against the outward expression of aggression when subjected to external forces demanding other-oriented aggression.

Case c in Figure 1 is unpredictable. While there is no internal ban against other-oriented aggression, neither is there a basis in strong external restraint for the legitimization of other-oriented aggression.

The feasibility of such experimentation has been demonstrated recently by King.[1] He found that persons who verbalized anger against the experimenter in response to frustration experienced cardiovascular changes similar to those produced by nor-epinephrine while those who expressed anger against themselves experienced cardiovascular changes similar to those produced by epinephrine. Demonstration of the physiological concomitants of self-oriented and other-oriented aggression provides a means of measuring with considerable objectivity the subject's reaction to frustration.

If we are willing to assume that subjects carry with them into the experimental situation the system of demands and expectations appropriate to their status and relational positions, we may introduce tests of our formulation of Part II. This procedure, holding constant all aspects of the experimental situation, must be distinguished from that used in recent suggestive research showing that less intense aggression was directed toward an instigator of higher status than the subject as compared with aggression directed toward an instigator of lower status than the subject.[2] Procedural design varying the relative status position of the instigator of the frustration would not reflect the degree to which the behavior of the subject is accustomed to conform to the demands and expectations of other persons.

By ranking subjects on the variables of status and strength of the relational system—holding constant the strength of internal prohibitions against the outward expression of aggression—we would be able to test our prediction that persons with high status and weak relational system would have the highest "sociological probability" of self-oriented aggression in response to the experimental frustration while persons with low status and a strong relational system would have the highest probability of other-oriented aggression. Negroes could be compared with whites, males with females, etc. Similarly, those with strong relational systems—the married, the club member and the person with many friends—could be compared with a group of persons isolated from meaningful relationships with other persons.

A number of additional testable hypotheses have been generated in the course of development of the argument.

The data of Part I were interpreted tentatively as a function of differences in frustration experienced by high and low status categories during expansion and contraction phases of the business cycle. The relationship between suicide, homicide and the business cycle, with status held constant, indicated that high status categories experience frustration during contractions in business while the lowest status category experiences frustration during expansions in business. This hypothesis may be tested by research through time on the vertical mobility patterns of a high status and low status group and the subjective attitudes expressed during the phases of the business cycle. We would predict that attitudes reflecting frustration and deprivation would be prominent in the high status group during business contraction and that the same attitudes would be expressed by the low status group during periods of business expansion.

We used the general positive association between suicide and status and the general negative association between homicide and status as the basis of an assumption that persons committing suicide within each gross ascriptive category are recruited from the upper classes within the category and that persons committing homicide within each gross ascriptive category are recruited from the lower classes within the category. This assumption should be tested by examination of certificates of death by suicide and the examination of detailed police records on murderers. We would predict that Negroes who commit homicide are concentrated disproportionately in the lower classes of the Negro community while Negroes who commit suicide are concentrated disproportionately in the upper classes of the Negro community.

At two different points in the argument we based our interpretation on an assumed high status position of the female within the Negro community. The correlation between suicide of Negro females and the business cycle was as high as the correlation between suicide of Negro males and the business cycle. This "contradiction" to the general pattern of highest correlations for highest status categories was tentatively interpreted as a function of the high prestige of the Negro female as compared with the Negro male. Similarly in Part II, the concentration of homicide among males was interpreted in part as a function of the fact that homicide is concentrated disproportionately among Negroes and that Negro males were of lower status than Negro females. If homicide is concentrated among lower status categories—and if males within the Negro community hold a prestige position lower on the average than females—the empirical result of high rates of homicide among males would be rationalized.

This hypothesis may be tested by research comparing the ratios of male to female homicide among the white and Negro categories. If our interpretation is correct, we would expect the ratio of male to female murderers among Negroes to exceed the ratio of male to female murderers among whites. Further research on the status position of the female in the Negro family is also needed.

Our theoretical formulation predicts that the homicide rate among the married, holding age constant, will be greater than the homicide rate among the unmarried. This hypothesis was suggested by the positive relationship between homicide and strength of the relational system. Examination of police and criminal records will provide adequate test of the hypothesis.

Research directed at the concentration of suicide and homicide within the central disorganized sectors of cities would permit test of the hypothesis that the high suicide rate is accounted for by persons with minimal involvement in meaningful relationships with others while the high homicide rate occurs among the ethnic groupings and as part of the operation of the "underworld." We have suggested that the subordinate status position of the ethnic categories in these areas and the tight social control of the deviant underworld converge to increase the degree of external restraint over behavior and legitimize the expression of aggression against others.

We were led to our formulation of the strength of the relational system as a second form of external restraint by the denial of the research hypothesis that the persons past 65 would have a lower suicide rate than younger persons because of the loss of status position with retirement. Despite the lowered status position of the aged person in modern society, the probability of suicide is at its maximum. This contradiction to the general positive association between suicide and status position led us to the hypothesis that the variables of status and strength of the relational system were operating in opposite directions in the case of age. In the search for an explanation of why the strength of the relational system decreases with age, we were led to the hypothesis that suicide rises with age because the probability of "orphanage" rises with age. Test of the hypothesis would involve the computation of suicide rates among a group with parents surviving and a group with parents dead, holding the effect of age and marital status constant. We would predict that the group with parents dead would have a higher suicide rate than the group with parents living because the group with dead parents would be operating under a weaker system of relationships and consequent weaker external restraints. Our formulation would suggest that with the strength of the relational system held constant, the increase of suicide and the decrease of homicide with age would disappear. The operation of the status variable may result in a decline in suicide associated with the decline in status after age 65 when the strength of the relational system is controlled.

Each of the major points in the development of the argument should be tested independently. These include (1) the hypothesis that the strength of external restraint over behavior decreases as status position increases; (2) the hypothesis that the strength of external restraint over behavior decreases as the degree of involvement in social or cathectic relationships decreases; and (3) the hypothesis that the legitimization of other-oriented aggression increases with an increase in the strength of external restraint over behavior. Our final hypothesis can be tested experimentally as described in the opening of this Chapter. The second hypothesis is an accepted and fundamental assumption of sociological theory. The first hypothesis, that the strength of external restraint over behavior varies inversely with status position, can be tested in a number of relationships such as those of foreman-worker, employer-employee, relations between whites and Negroes, etc. The subjectively-experienced degree of external restraint of subordinate and superordinate categories may be compared.

Experimentation with the treatment of depressive mental patients would provide fertile ground for test of the proposition that the legitimization of other-oriented aggression varies positively with the strength of external restraint over behavior. If it is true that depressives are suffering from a "turning inward" of their aggressive energy, the imposition of rigid restraints upon their behavior would be expected to provide legitimization for the expression of aggression outwardly rather than against the self. And in the opposite case of the extremely aggressive mental patient, minimizing the degree of restraint imposed would be expected to weaken the legitimacy of the aggression.

Formulation of the psychological bases of legitimacy of other-oriented aggression has suggested certain additional hypotheses. The hypothesis that increased likelihood of loss of nurturance accounts for the associations between maternal dominance and guilt and between maternal dominance and epinephrine-like cardiovascular reaction during stress can be tested by seeing whether the relationships disappear when the degree of use of "love withdrawal" techniques of punishment by dominant mothers is held constant.

The associated hypothesis that subjects reacting during stress with nor-epinephrine-like cardiovascular patterns are subjects with low guilt can be tested by examination of differences in TAT and other projective measures of guilt taken on epinephrine-like and nor-epinephrine-like subjects. Confirmation or rejection of this hypothesis would aid in further exploration of possible physiological consequences of the process of internalization.

The hypothesis that persons who follow murder with suicide are persons who deprive themselves through the murder of a primary source of nurturance (as well as a primary source of frustration) may be tested by comparing the degree of positive attachment of murderer and victim prior to the homicide among those who later commit suicide and among those who do not commit suicide.

Finally, studies relating the value content of projections to the values of the parent providing at the same time primary nurturance and primary discipline during childhood would provide the empirical bridge for relating in conceptual terms the process of internalization and the process of projection.

APPENDICES

We shall limit discussion of previous research to those few studies which have either made important contributions to the conceptualization of suicide or have produced scientifically valid additions to the understanding of the relation of suicide and homicide with economic or sociological variables.

► SUICIDE: CONTRIBUTIONS TO THEORY

The most important theoretical contribution to the understanding of suicide appears in the work *Le Suicide* by Emile Durkheim. While Durkheim's work contains empirical data supporting his theory, the book is properly classified as a contribution to theory because of the fruitfulness of the concepts of "egoistic" and "anomic" suicide.

Durkheim used the concept of "anomie" to describe the effect of business cycles on suicide.

"In the case of economic disasters, indeed, something like a declassification occurs which suddenly casts certain individuals into a lower state than their previous one. Then they must reduce their requirements, restrain their needs, learn greater self-control. All the advantages of social influence are lost so far as they are concerned; their moral education has to be recommenced. But society cannot adjust them instantaneously to this new life and teach them to practice the increased self-repression to which they are unaccustomed. So they are not adjusted to the condition forced on them, and its very prospect is intolerable;

131

hence the suffering which detaches them from a reduced existence even before they have made a trial of it.

"It is the same if the source of the crisis is an abrupt growth of power and wealth. . . . With increased prosperity, desires increase. At the very moment when traditional rules have lost their authority, the richer prize offered these appetites stimulates them and makes them more exigent and impatient of control. . . .

". . . Above all, since this race for an unattainable goal can give no other pleasure but that of the race itself, if it is one, once it is interrupted the participants are left empty-handed. . . . All classes contend among themselves because no established classification any longer exists. . . . How could the desire to live not be weakened under such conditions?

"This explanation is confirmed by the remarkable immunity of poor countries. Poverty protects against suicide because it is a restraint in itself."[1]

Two further quotations from Durkheim clarify the concept of anomie.

"The enormous rate of those with independent means (720 per million) sufficiently shows that the possessors of most comfort suffer most. Everything that enforces subordination attenuates the effects of this state. At least the horizon of the lower classes is limited by those above them, and for this same reason their desires are more modest. Those who have only empty space above them are almost inevitably lost in it, if no force restrains them."[2]

The relevance of the concept of anomie for study of the relation of suicide and the business cycle is demonstrated in the following paragraph.

"If anomie never appeared except, as in the above instances, in intermittent spurts and acute crisis, it might cause the social suicide-rate to vary from time to time, but it would not be a regular, constant factor. In one sphere of social life, however—the sphere of trade and industry —it is actually in a chronic state."[3]

Durkheim's distinction between anomic and egoistic suicide is clarified in the next quotation.

"Certainly, this (anomic) and egoistic suicide have kindred ties. Both spring from society's insufficient presence in individuals. But the sphere of its absence is not the same in both cases. In egoistic suicide it is deficient in truly collective activity, thus depriving the latter of object and meaning. In anomic suicide, society's influence is lacking in the basically individual passions, thus leaving them without a check-rein.

In spite of their relationship, therefore, the two types are independent of each other. We may offer society everything social in us, and still be unable to control our desires: one may live in an anomic state without being egoistic, and vice versa. These two sorts of suicide, therefore, do not draw their chief recruits from the same social environments; one has its principal field among intellectual careers, . . . the other, the industrial or commercial world."[4]

While he attributes egoistic suicide to "excessive individuation" or detachment from society, Durkheim's altruistic suicide is attributed to the opposite cause of "insufficient individuation."

Halbwachs' reworking of Durkheim's statistical data attempted to reduce all types of suicide to a single explanation, the result of the detachment of the individual from participation in society.[5]

Further theoretical insights about suicide have come from the writings of the psychoanalysts. Menninger, in *Man Against Himself*, notes the element of aggression in suicide.

"It is not difficult to discover in the act of suicide the existence of various elements. First of all it is a *murder*. . . . But suicide is also a murder by the self. It is a death in which are combined in one person the murderer and the murdered."[6]

At another point Menninger states that the "theory of suicide is that the wish to kill, unexpectedly robbed of certain external occasions or objects of unconscious gratification, may be turned back upon the person of the 'wisher' and carried into effect as suicide."[7]

Fenichel, in summarizing the psychoanalytic work on suicide, describes an additional element, the presence of a punishing conscience or "superego."

"The suicide of the depressed patient is, if examined from the standpoint of the superego, a turning of sadism against the person himself, and the thesis that nobody kills himself who had not intended to kill somebody else is proved by the depressive suicide. From the standpoint of the ego, suicide is, first of all, an expression of the fact that the terrible tension the pressure of the superego induces has become unbearable. Frequently the passive thought of giving up any active fighting seems to express itself; the loss of self-esteem is so complete that any hope of regaining it is abandoned. . . . To have a desire to live evidently means to feel a certain self-esteem, to feel supported by the protective forces of a superego. . . .

"Other suicidal acts have a much more active character. They assert themselves as desperate attempts to enforce, at any cost, the cessation

of the pressure of the superego. They are the most extreme acts of
ingratiatory submission to punishment and to the superego's cruelty;
simultaneously they are also the most extreme acts of rebellion, that
is, murder—murder of the original objects whose incorporation created
the superego, murder, it is true, of the kind of Dorian Gray's murder
of his image."[8]

▶ CONTRIBUTIONS OF FACT

Ogburn, Thomas, and Dublin and Bunzel have demonstrated the
existence of a high negative relationship between suicide and the
business cycle.

Ogburn and Thomas constructed a composite index of the business cycle, made up of nine separate business series.[9] Thomas summarizes the findings as follows:

"The suicide rate would be expected, we think, to vary with business prosperity and business depression, and so it does. We have taken
the suicide rate as computed by Hoffman (Frederick L. Hoffman, 'Suicide Record for 1920,' *Spectator,* March 9, 1922) for one hundred
cities of the United States for 1900-1920, and correlated the suicide
cycles (measured from the trend line $Y = 20.35 + 0.171x — 0.0656x^2
— 0.00348x^3$) with cycles of business conditions for the same period,
and we find a correlation of —0.74 ± 0.07."[10]

Thomas' study of the relation between business cycles and social
conditions in England and Wales yielded similar results.

"The coefficient of correlation for the whole period, 1858-1913, is
—.50 for synchronous items, and —.47 for a lag of one year."[11]

Dublin and Bunzel have confirmed these findings.

"The coefficient of correlation between the monthly business index
and the monthly suicide index during the period of years 1910-1931
has been computed by the usual technique, and is found to be relatively high, namely, —.47 ± .05. The correlation here is about the
same as that between body weight and height found in adult males."[12]

Dublin and Bunzel found that the suicide rate for white males in
the United States Death Registration Area was correlated more
highly with their business index than the rate for white females. The
coefficient for white males is —.66±.13 and —.44±.18 for white
females.[13]

Research on the ecological distribution of suicide by Cavan and

Schmid has demonstrated that suicide rates are higher in the central, disorganized sections of large cities than in outlying residential areas.

Cavan was able to isolate four high suicide rate areas in Chicago during the period 1919-1921; the Loop and its periphery of cheap hotels for men; the Lower North Side which includes a shifting population in the rooming house area; the Near South Side with one-fourth of its population Negro; and the West Madison Street area of "homeless" men. Cavan found that the high suicide rate areas tend to be areas of extreme social and personal disorganization.[14]

Schmid's studies of the ecology of suicide in Seattle and Minneapolis confirm the findings of Cavan that suicide tends to be concentrated in the central, disorganized sections of large cities.[15] These studies relate suicide to high rates of residential mobility and the failure of social norms to control individual behavior in areas of social disorganization.

There are certain differences in absolute rates of suicide for each status category in the United States at a given point in time.

1. The suicide rate increases with age. Suicide rates of all persons aged 65 and over are roughly three times as high as suicide rates for all persons in the age brackets under 45 years. Similarly, rates of the single, married, and divorced categories are roughly three times as high in the age groups over 65 as they are in the age groups under 45. While suicide rates of the widowed are slightly higher in the upper age brackets than in the younger brackets, the increase with age is much less marked than in the case of the married, the single, and the divorced. These data are shown graphically in Figure 1.

2. The rate for males is higher than the rate for females. Within the United States, for the year 1940, the rate for males in the younger age groupings was roughly three times that for females. In the older age groupings, the ratio of male to female suicide was yet higher.[16]

3. The rate for white persons is higher than the rate for non-white persons. The rate per 100,000 for white persons in the United States in 1940 was 15.5. For all other races it was 4.6 per 100,000. The ratio of white to non-white suicide grows larger with increasing age.[17]

4. The rate for officers in the United States Army is higher than the rate for enlisted men. In 12 of the 16 years from 1914 to 1929, the suicide rate for officers was higher than that for enlisted men.[18]

5. The suicide rate is higher in urban than in rural areas. In

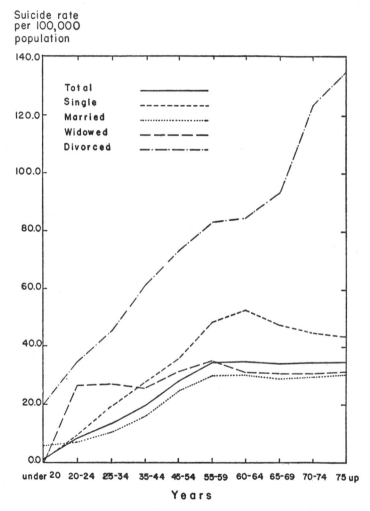

Figure 1. Suicide per 100,000 Enumerated Population by Age and Marital Status, 1940 (Source: *Vital Statistics—Special Reports*, October 1947, p. 162).

United States cities of over 100,000 population, the suicide rate in 1940 was 16.8. In cities between 10,000 and 100,000 population it was 15.6, dropping to 12.0 in rural areas.[19]

6. The suicide rate of married persons, holding the effect of age constant, is lower than the suicide rate of the single, the widowed and the divorced. For each grouping over 20 years, the frequency of suicide of married persons is lower than among single, widowed, and divorced persons in the same age group.[20]

7. Suicide and economic status are also closely related. In summarizing data on suicide rates by social class in England and Wales, Dublin and Bunzel state:

"The British figures ostensibly support the claim that among those who are engaged in the work of the world, suicide occurs most frequently among the more well-to-do. But among the laboring classes, skilled and unskilled, suicide is most frequent among those nearest the poverty line, and especially is this true at the more advanced ages of life. Hence suicide appears to predominate at both extremes of the social scale, although largely, it is true, at the upper end."[21]

In summarizing United States data Dublin and Bunzel report: (1) more suicide among Industrial Insurance Policy holders than among Ordinary Insurance Policy holders; (2) suicide ranks higher as a cause of death among large policy holders than among smaller policy holders and higher as a cause of death among small policy holders than among the general population. They conclude that their data "incomplete as they are, appear, in general, to harmonize with the British study in showing that suicide predominates at both ends of the social and financial scale, although chiefly at the upper end."[22]

8. In a study by one of the authors, the suicide rate in the 14 all-white community areas in Chicago with the highest median rentals was found to be lower than the rate in the 13 all-white areas with the lowest median rentals in both of the periods from 1930-1932 and 1939-1941.[23]

While Durkheim had examined certain of the empirical uniformities in the incidence of suicide and homicide in varying social categories, he rejected the idea that there might be some fundamental theoretical connection between these two acts.[24] But a recent and stimulating study by Porterfield has re-opened the question.

While Porterfield fails to distinguish between crimes against persons and crimes against property, he concludes that "areas with high suicide and low crime rates are high in social status . . ." and "areas of low suicide and high crime rates have low scores for social status. . . ."[25] Porterfield's conclusion, strengthened by additional data presented in Part II, provides one of the important foundations for our analysis.

► CRIME: CONTRIBUTIONS TO THEORY

The theoretical basis of research into the relation between crime and economic conditions, like research into other social "aspects" of the business cycle, has been largely the theory of "social forces" and their impact upon human behavior.[26] Business cycles have been viewed as impersonal forces operating in society and influencing human conduct in many ways. Research has emphasized the relation between these social forces and human behavior, i.e., the amount of concurrence in the fluctuations of certain social conditions and the fluctuations in business conditions. Writers have been cautious in suggesting causal relationships and have referred instead to "social aspects of" or "connections between" social forces and human behavior. Dorothy Thomas, for example, makes no attempt to present an integrated theoretical statement as a basis for her research into the "Social Aspects of the Business Cycle." Throughout her volume, references are made to subjective feelings of optimism or pessimism, to increases or decreases in the consumption of alcohol, and to economic need as factors accounting for the relation of crime and the business cycle.

An exception to the usual social forces theory is found in the work of William A. Bonger.[27] Writing in the Marxist tradition, Bonger reduces the causes of crime to one underlying factor—the economic pressures of a capitalistic system. The works of Bonger, Dennis[28] and other writers prior to 1922 leads one to agree with Thomas' observation that "A review of the literature on the subject suggests that discussions of the relations between crime and economic conditions are still in the realm of metaphysics."[29]

▶ CONTRIBUTIONS OF FACT

In 1922, Ogburn and Thomas found a coefficient of correlation of
—.35 between a business cycle index of their own construction and
a crime index comprised of the number of convictions for criminal
offenses in the courts of record of the state of New York for the
period, 1870-1920.[30] Davies found a correlation of +.41 between
annual admissions to New York State prisons and an index of
wholesale prices for the period, 1896-1915.[31] Ogburn and Thomas
also found a low negative correlation (—.12) between the business
cycle and the "number of convictions for offenses against the person, exclusive of offenses against property with violence."

In 1925 Thomas published the results of her study using British
data, a study which remains the most thorough in the field. She summarizes her findings relative to the crimes upon which our attention
is focused in the following way.

"Crimes against the person and against morals show slight tendencies
to increase in prosperity, suggesting the possible influence of alcoholism
upon such crimes. Changes in law, etc., have made these series somewhat unreliable for long time comparisons."[32]

Thomas' conclusions have been generally accepted and the matter
has been allowed to rest.

Radzinowicz has made a very thorough analysis of the influence
of economic conditions on crime in Poland for the period, 1927-
1934. His "business cycle" is limited to a single peak and a single
trough. His primary contribution lies in the selection of economic
indices which seem appropriate for specific crimes. On the basis of
graphic comparisons of series, his somewhat over-generalized conclusions are as follows:

". . . the parallelism ascertained between offenses against property
and economic conditions . . . established without any doubt that there
is a causal relationship between the two phenomena in the sense that
changes which have occurred in the volume of these offenses have been
determined by changes in economic conditions.

"Our investigations lead us to suppose that the coefficient of crime
particular to a certain social group tends to increase not so much when
the general economic level of this group is low, but rather when the

economic status of that social group drops violently and rapidly. . . . in general, prosperous times are less effective in reducing crime than times of crisis in increasing it. As offenses against property are mostly committed by those classes of society which normally border on the poverty line, even a slight deterioration in their economic situation puts these classes in exceptionally dire straits and leads to an increase of their ratio of crime. On the other hand, there must be exceptionally great and prolonged prosperity if it is to react on the economic, moral, and psychological position of these classes, and in consequence contribute to a decrease in their crime ratio. Prosperity, in order to influence the downward trend of crime, must be especially marked when it follows a period of violent depression."[33]

Radzinowicz notes the tendency for crimes against the person to rise during periods of prosperity and remarks that the "curve (of these crimes) follows closely that of the consumption of alcohol."[34]

A number of studies have been carried on in the United States which tend to substantiate the findings already reported. These studies are all for more limited jurisdictions and in several cases represent very short periods of time.[35]

Interest in the relation of crime and suicide with the business cycle has lagged in recent years, a lag which may well be due to the lack of a theory which would make explicit the dynamics of the relationship between economic forces and psychological acts of suicide and homicide.

appendix II

CORRELATION OF TIME SERIES

—TRENDS AND CYCLES

The methods employed by Ogburn and Thomas, and the Burns-Mitchell technique,[1] are followed in the present study. Trend lines are fitted by the least squares method to time series of the economic index and our series of suicide and homicide, thus isolating fluctuations which are then correlated by the Pearsonian method. The measures so obtained are not interpreted as indicating "exact" or "true" relationships. The trend lines fitted to the data represent, rather, "brief summaries of the movements during the period studied, useful for interpolation."[2] Coefficients of correlation have the advantage of objectivity and they indicate relative relationships within the context of comparable factors of time, population, and uniform reporting systems.

▶ THE BUSINESS CYCLE

Wesley Mitchell's research into business cycles led him to define business cycles as "a species of fluctuations in the economic activities of organized communities."[3] The measurement of business cycles and the analysis of the factors involved in these fluctuations have become a major field of interest for the economists. As a result of this interest and the research which it has stimulated, the sociologist has available an abundance of economic data for research into the "social aspects of the business cycle."

141

The economic factor employed in the present study is the Cleveland Trust Company's index of "American Business Activity Since 1790," commonly referred to as "Ayres' Index" because Leonard P. Ayres developed the index.[4] Ayres' index exhibits substantial conformity to the analysis of business cycles in the United States presented by the National Bureau of Economic Research.[5] It has the further advantage that it is available in convenient form for the type of analysis followed in this research.

▶ THE CONCEPTS OF TRENDS AND CYCLES

Trends, trend lines, and cycles require additional comment. The object of this research is to investigate the relation of the short term fluctuations of business activity, called business cycles, and the fluctuations of various social phenomena. Whereas the existence of cycles of social phenomena has not been demonstrated empirically to our satisfaction,[6] we wish to isolate such fluctuations as do occur. In order to isolate these fluctuations, it is necessary to eliminate the long term trends of these phenomena. One method of doing this is to fit a mathematical trend line to a series of data and compute the deviations from this trend. The deviations can then be statistically correlated, and a measure of the relation of the two variables obtained. Thus, while it is not the purpose of this research to study the trends, per se, of business activity and social phenomena, such trends must be established in order to isolate the cyclical fluctuations which we wish to examine.

The dictionary definition of "trend" is a "general course or direction; bent."[7] When dealing with time series the concept of trend, sometimes called "secular trend," thus refers to long term movements of the data. The general course of time series will vary in form. The trend of a series may be described by a straight line or a parabola, or by some other equation.

It may be that a single trend does not characterize a series of data. Such is the case when the movement of data changes direction abruptly and continues in the general direction of the change. A new trend has been established.

It is important to make clear the distinction between the trend of the data and their fluctuations. Mathematically, a line can be fitted to a time series which will pass through each point of the data. Such a line would not constitute a trend line, for it would not reflect the general movement of the data. Fluctuations would not be isolated, but eliminated. Generally, then, a trend line should not change direction abruptly.

What sort of line should be drawn through a series of data? Various lines might be drawn. When treating the business cycle, however, two criteria emerge to aid the researcher.

First of all, when fitting a trend line to the index of business activity, the fluctuations about that trend must conform to reality. The years in which peaks of prosperity and troughs of depression occur are generally agreed upon. They have been the subject of intensive investigation for many years and in many countries. The work of the National Bureau of Economic Research includes a list of the peaks and troughs of the business cycle in the United States from 1834 to 1938.[8] Trend lines should cut the business series at points approximately midway between these turning points. That is, the fluctuations isolated by fitting a trend to a particular series of business must conform to the reality of the peaks and troughs of prosperity and depression which have been established by past research.

The second criterion to be met when fitting a trend line is that the line must actually be a trend, a general movement, as discussed above. This requires that the series comprise a long enough period to constitute a trend, rather than simply describing a short term movement or fluctuation.

▶ TRENDS IN SOCIAL PHENOMENA

When fitting a trend line to a series of social phenomena, the idea is somewhat different. We must assume the existence of cycles of social phenomena. Unlike the business cycle, there are no generally agreed upon turning points, no peaks or troughs of social phenomena, to which reference can be made. Since our problem is the investigation of the relation between social phenomena and the business cycle, we attack the problem of trends in social series by again making reference to the turning points in the business cycle. If there is any relation between these variables, this relation should be reflected about the turning points. If the trend line is made to cut the social series at points midway between the turning points of the business cycle, the relation between the two variables will be maximized. By thus maximizing the correlation between each social series and the business cycle we will be better able to judge the nature of the relation between these phenomena.

Here again, the second criterion holds true. There must be sufficient years in the series to constitute a trend. This is often a major problem in this research, due to the unavailability of long social series of the type in which we are interested.

These principles are sometimes difficult to follow because of the small number of years included in parts of this study and because some social phenomena bear little or no relation to the business cycle. In an effort to fully exploit the data and to saisfy the criteria for trend analysis, more than one trend line has often been fitted to a series of data.

► LARGE AND SMALL CYCLES

We have indicated that the fluctuations of any series of data about its long term trend are called cycles. We speak of the business cycle as consisting of periods of prosperity when business fluctuations are found to be above the trend of business activity, and depression when business fluctuations are below this trend.

A further distinction can be made between large and small cycles. We commonly refer to the "depression of the 'thirties' " as being part of the large cycle extending from the peak of prosperity in 1929 to the war-time peak in 1943. According to this notion, the years between 1930 and 1940 are regarded as being a spectacularly long sweep of business depression, in contrast to the comparative prosperity of the 1920's and war-time prosperity of the 1940's. The years 1930 through 1939 are all below the long term trend of American business activity from 1790 to the present. A straight line fitted to our business index for the years, 1929-41/46-49, places all of the 1930's, with the exception of 1930 and 1931, below the trend line. Figure 1 presents this picture.

Number

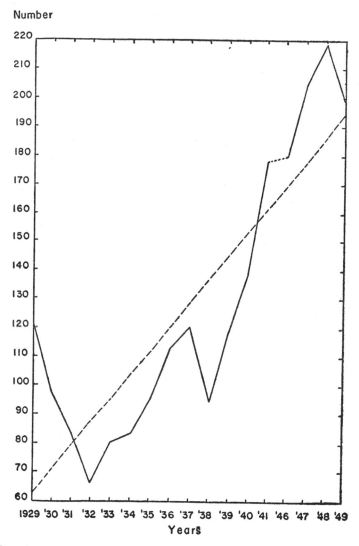

Figure 1. Ayres' Index of Business Activity, Fitted to Cut Off Cycles, 1929-41/46-49:
$$X_1 = 128.7471 + 28.2096X$$

Closer inspection of the data indicates that the years between 1930 and 1940 were not uniformly "bad" years. The extent of depression varied considerably from year to year. Thus, referring to our index, we find that 1937 was 57.3 points above the trough year of 1932. So the year 1937 may be regarded as a minor peak. Furthermore, the year 1938 was some 26.2 points below the 1937 figure and constitutes a minor trough. A smaller cycle thus exists within the larger, more pronounced cycle.

It is the "small" cycle analysis to which we customarily refer when we speak of the business cycle. The National Bureau of Economic Research includes 1937 as a business cycle peak and 1938 as a business cycle trough, in the United States.

The technique used to discriminate between large and small cycles is that of fitting different trend lines to the data. We have seen that when a straight line is fitted to Ayres' index for the years 1929-41/46-49, 1937 is indicated as a depression year. If a second degree parabola is fitted to these data, 1937 becomes a peak, and 1935 and 1936 are likewise indicated as years of relative prosperity, though 1935 is only slightly above the trend line (Figure 2).

Table 1—Business Indices and Equations of Trend Lines

Correlated with Series[a]	Area	Trend
1,2; Table 2	U.S.[b]	1900-1909: $Y_1 = 51.6449 + 2.2030Y - .1812Y^2$
		1910-16/1919-41/1946-47: $Y_1 = 100.3000 + 2.7852Y$
3-6, 25-26; Table 2	U.S.[b]	1923-41/1946-47: $Y_1 = 114.2619 + 3.4686Y$
7-18; Table 2	U.S.[b]	1920-41/1946-47: $Y_1 = 109.9458 + 3.2655Y$
19,20; Table 2	U.S.[b]	1910-16/1919-41/1946-47: $Y_1 = 100.3000 + 2.7852Y$
21,22; Table 2	U.S.[b]	1910-16/1919-38: $Y_1 = 88.5222 + 1.4020Y$
23,24; Table 2	U.S.[b]	1923-1938: $Y_1 = 98.7500 - .4374Y$
27,28; Table 2	U.S.[b]	1905-1909: $Y_1 = 56.4200 + .3500Y$
		1910-16/1919-41/1946-47: $Y_1 = 100.3000 + 2.7852Y$

a. Refers to number of series in Table 2 in this Appendix.
b "American Business Activity Since 1790," The Cleveland Trust Co. (Cleveland: 1949), p. 1.

By fitting similar trend lines to social series wherever possible, the fluctuations of small social cycles can be correlated with the small fluctuations of business, and the large business cycle fluctuations can be correlated with large social cycles. In this manner we can test the relation between large and small cycles of social phenomena and the business cycle and better understand the nature of this relation.

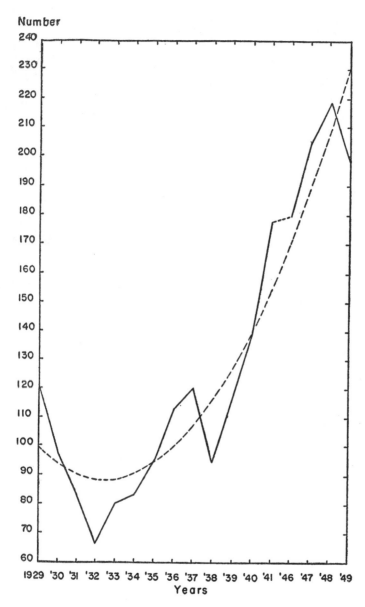

Figure 2. Ayres' Index of Business Activity, Fitted to Cut Off Small Cycles, 1929-41/46-49: $X_1 = 107.0294 + 8.2096X + .9049X^2$.

Table 2—Equations of Trend Lines Fitted to Suicide Time Series

1. Males, U.S.D.R.S. (42 years).
   1900-1910:
   $X_1 = 19.7000 + 1.0191X$
   1911-16/1919-22:
   $X_1 = 20.3949 - .9582X - .0223X^2$
   1923-41/1946-47:
   $X_1 = 21.2810 + .0588X$

2. Females, U.S.D.R.S. (42 years).
   1900-1913:
   $X_1 = 6.7685 + .2134X - .0196X^2$
   1914-16/1919-21:
   $X_1 = 6.4429 - .3750X$
   1923-41/1946-47:
   $X_1 = 6.4429 + .0153X$

3. White Males, U.S.D.R.S. (21 years).
   1923-41/1946-47:
   $X_1 = 22.7952 + .0739X$

4. White Females, U.S.D.R.S. (21 years).
   1923-41/1946-47:
   $X_1 = 6.9157 + .0236X$

5. Non-White Males, U.S.D.R.S. (21 years).
   1923-41/1946-47:
   $X_1 = 7.1143 + .0137X$

6. Non-White Females, U.S.D.R.S.
   (21 years).
   1923-41/1946-47:
   $X_1 = 2.3029 - .0152X$

7. Males 15-24, U.S.D.R.S. (24 years).
   1920-41/1946-47:
   $X_1 = 8.0458 + .0349X$

8. Females 15-24, U.S.D.R.S. (24 years).
   1920-41/1946-47:
   $X_1 = 4.9667 - .0928X$

9. Males 25-34, U.S.D.R.S. (24 years).
   1920-41/1946-47:
   $X_1 = 18.2833 + .0547X$

10. Females 25-34, U.S.D.R.S. (24 years).
    1920-41/1946-47:
    $X_1 = 8.0875 - .0253X$

11. Males 35-44, U.S.D.R.S. (24 years).
    1920-41/1946-47:
    $X_1 = 28.2833 - .0064X$

12. Females 35-44, U.S.D.R.S. (24 years).
    1920-41/1946-47:
    $X_1 = 9.8158 + .0303X$

13. Males 45-54, U.S.D.R.S. (24 years).
    1920-41/1946-47:
    $X_1 = 42.1500 + .0546X$

14. Females 45-54, U.S.D.R.S. (24 years).
    1920-41/1946-47:
    $X_1 = 12.0479 + .0784X$

15. Males 55-64, U.S.D.R.S. (24 years).
    1920-41/1946-47:
    $X_1 = 54.6167 + .1896X$

16. Females 55-64, U.S.D.R.S. (24 years).
    1920-41/1946-47:
    $X_1 = 12.3583 + .0340X$

17. Males 65-74, U.S.D.R.S. (24 years).
    1920-41/1946-47:
    $X_1 = 61.5042 - .0124X$

18. Females 65-74, U.S.D.R.S. (24 years).
    1920-41/1946-47:
    $X_1 = 269.6250 + 11.5178X$

19. White, U.S.D.R.S. (32 years).
    1910-16/1919-22:
    $X_1 = 14.9053 - .4582X - .0478X^2$
    1923-41/1946-47:
    $X_1 = 14.9476 + .0427X$

20. Non-White, U.S.D.R.S. (32 years).
    1910-16/1919-23:
    $X_1 = 6.7241 - .8724X + .0462X^2$

21. Urban White, U.S.D.R.S. (27 years).
    1910-16/1919-22:
    $X_1 = 5388.3360 + 104.9364X - 3.9336X^2$
    1923-1938:
    $X_1 = 9877.9330 + 271.6897X - 40.0292X^2$

Table 2—continued

22. Urban Colored, U.S.D.R.S. (27 years).
   1910-16/1919-22:
   $X_1 = 143.5547 + 8.7818X - .8718X^2$
   1923-1938:
   $X_1 = 381.6184 + 11.8000X - 1.8291X^2$

23. Rural White, U.S.D.R.S. (16 years).
   1923-1938:
   $X_1 = 7481.8565 + 310.9779X - 17.9256X^2$

24. Rural Colored, U.S.D.R.S. (16 years).
   1923-1938:
   $X_1 = 232.0839 + 11.3603X - .8363X^2$

25. White, U.S.D.R.S. (21 years).
   1923-41/1946-47:
   $X_1 = 14.9476 + .0427X$

26. Non-White, U.S.D.R.S. (21 years).
   1923-41/1946-47:
   $X_1 = 4.5952 - .0036X$

27. Married, Cook County, Illinois
   (37 years).
   1905-1916:
   $X_1 = 285.6667 + 12.2448X$
   1919-41/1946-47:
   $X_1 = 310.6800 + 1.2185X$

28. Single, Cook County, Illinois
   (37 years).
   1905-16/1919-22:
   $X_1 = 151.9111 + .1676X - .7017X^2$
   1923-41/1946-47:
   $X_1 = 128.333 - 1.1494X$

The distinction between large and small cycles is made in this volume only in our discussion of the gross relation between crime and the business cycle. This is done in an experimental sense since this distinction is not conventionally made in research of this type.

Table 3—Business Indices and Equations of Trend Lines[a]

No. of Index[b]		Trend Line	Size of Cycle
1.	1929-41/46-49:	$X_1 = 128.7471 + 8.2096x$	Large
2.	1929-41/46-49:	$X_1 = 107.0294 + 8.2096x + .9049x^2$	Small
3.	1929-41:	$X_1 = 106.7846 + 4.8786x$	Small
4.	1930-41/46-49:	$X_1 = 129.2563 + 9.6466x$	Large
5.	1930-41/46-49:	$X_1 = 114.0731 + 9.6466x + .7145x^2$	Small
6.	1930-41:	$X_1 = 105.6338 + 6.8371x$	Small
7.	1925-41:	$X_1 = 87.3298 + 2.1500x + .8191x^2$	Small
8.	1925-41:	$X_1 = 106.9882 + .2150x$	Small
9.	1928-41/46-49:	$X_1 = 127.8167 + 7.2063x$	Large
10.	1928-41/46-49:	$X_1 = 102.8057 + 7.2063x + .9292x^2$	Small
11.	1910-16:	$X_1 = 69.6430 + 3.2320x$	
	1919-40:	$X_1 = 98.1727 + 1.2438x$	Small
12.	1920-40:	$X_1 = 98.8762 + 1.21987x$	Small
13.	1910-16:	$X_1 = 69.6430 + 3.2320x$	
	1919/1921-40:	$X_1 = 98.6762 + 1.2744x$	Small
14.	1918/19-1940/41:	$X_1 = -103.000 - 9.8132x$	Small
15.	1926-41:	$X_1 = 107.2000 + 2.4953x$	Small
16.	1926-41:	$X_1 = 86.1970 + 2.4953x + .9884x^2$	Small

a. "American Business Activity Since 1790," The Cleveland Trust Co. (Cleveland, 1950), p. 1.
b. Business indices with which crime series are correlated in Chapter III and Appendix V. (See Table 4 for crime series).

Table 4—Equations of Trend Lines Fitted to Crime Time Series[a]

1. Murder, 11 cities, large cycles (17 years).
   1929-41/46-49:
   $X_1 = 706.6471 - 8.3407x$ (1)

2. Murder, 11 cities, small cycles (17 years).
   1929-36:
   $X_1 = 795.0623 - 29.7619x$
   $- 6.8214x^2$
   1937-41/46-49:
   $X_1 = 648.9695 + 23.7333x$
   $+ 1.6379x^2$ (2)

3. Murder, 11 cities, small cycles (13 years).
   1929-41:
   $X_1 = 682.5809 - 24.4066x$
   $+ 1.0629x^2$ (3)

4. Murder, 55 cities, large cycles (16 years).
   1930-41/46-49:
   $X_1 = 950.3750 - 6.9794x$ (4)

5. Murder, 55 cities, small cycles (16 years).
   1930-36:
   $X_1 = 1053.1428 - 1.3571x$
   $- 12.2857x^2$
   1937-41/46-49:
   $X_1 = 908.6667 + 11.1333x$ (5)

6. Murder, 55 cities, small cycles (12 years).
   1930-41:
   $X_1 = 974.5482 - 19.8497x$
   $- 2.7523x^2$ (6)

7. Murder, Los Angeles, small cycles (17 years).
   1925-41:
   $X_1 = 77.5072 + 2.0074x$
   $- .3128x^2$ (7)

8. Murder, Baltimore, large cycles (18 years).
   1928-41/46-49:
   $X_1 = 71.6667 + 2.2456x$ (9)

9. Murder, Baltimore, small cycles (18 years).
   1928-41/46-49:
   $X_1 = 63.3494 + 2.2456x + .3090x^2$ (10)

10. Aggravated assault, 9 cities, large cycles (17 years).
    1929-41/46-49:
    $X_1 = 3416.2941 + 297.4289x$ (1)

11. Aggravated assault, 9 cities, small cycles (17 years).
    1929-36:
    $X_1 = 2357.6250 + 24.7262x$ (2)

12. Aggravated assault, 9 cities, small cycles (13 years).
    1929-41:
    $X_1 = 2353.8461 + 9.6209x$ (3)

13. Aggravated assault, 53 cities, large cycles (16 years).
    1930-41/46-49:
    $X_1 = 8432.8750 + 495.0118x$ (4)

14. Aggravated assault, 53 cities, small cycles (16 years).
    1930-35:
    $X_1 = 6574.6660 + 189.7714x$
    1936-41/46-49:
    $X_1 = 7993.6800 + 919.0303x$
    $+ 188.3787x^2$ (5)

15. Aggravated assault, 53 cities, small cycles (12 years).
    1930-41:
    $X_1 = 7071.1412 + 93.5350x$
    $- 14.7601x^2$ (6)

16. Aggravated assault, Los Angeles, large cycles (17 years).
    1925-41:
    $X_1 = 435.5882 + 19.5000x$ (8)

17. Aggravated assault, Los Angeles, small cycles (17 years).
    1925-41:
    $X_1 = 390.1274 + 19.5000x$
    $+ 1.8942x^2$ (7)

Table 4—continued

18. Aggravated assault, Portland, Oregon, large cycles (17 years).

1925-41:
$$X_1 = 47.5294 + 1.2745x \quad (8)$$

19. Aggravated assault, Portland, Oregon, small cycles (17 years).

1925-41:
$$X_1 = 56.0806 + 1.2745x - .3563x^2 \quad (7)$$

20. Aggravated assault, Buffalo, large cycles (18 years).

1928-41/46-49:
$$X_1 = 274.2220 - 20.9124x \quad (9)$$

21. Aggravated assault, Buffalo, small cycles (18 years).

1928-34:
$$X_1 = 424.9524 - 4.4643x + .0119x^2$$
1935-41/46-49:
$$X_1 = 156.0587 - .6545x + 2.2214x^2 \quad (10)$$

22. Aggravated assault, Rochester, large cycles (18 years).

1928-41/46-49:
$$X_1 = 44.1667 + 1.9123x \quad (9)$$

23. Aggravated assault, Rochester, small cycles (18 years).

1928-36:
$$X_1 = 41.2818 + 4.6000x - .3756x^2$$
1937-41/46-49:
$$X_1 = 49.5556 + 3.5667x \quad (10)$$

24. Deaths by alcoholism, U.S.D.R.S. (13 years).

1929-41:
$$X_1 = 3304.5942 - 141.8626x - .9875x^2 \quad (3)$$

25. Deaths by homicide, white, U.S.D.R.S. of 1900 (29 years).

1910-16:
$$X_1 = 3.7860 + .0110x$$
1919-40:
$$X_1 = 3.8800 - .0830x + .0380x^2 \quad (11)$$

26. Deaths by homicide, white, U.S.D.R.S. of 1900 (28 years).

1910-16:
$$X_1 = 3.7860 + .0110x$$
1919/1921-40:
$$X_1 = 3.8538 - .0921x - .0121x^2 \quad (13)[b]$$

27. Deaths by homicide, non-white, U.S.D.R.S. of 1900 (29 years).

1910-16:
$$X_1 = 20.4700 - .4464x$$
1919-40:
$$X_1 = 39.1000 - .2740x - .1598x^2 \quad (11)$$

28. Deaths by homicide, non-white, U.S.D.R.S. of 1900 (28 years).

1910-16:
$$X_1 = 20.4700 - .4464x$$
1919/1921-40:
$$X_1 = 39.0142 - .4119x - .1645x^2 \quad (13)[b]$$

29. Deaths by homicide, white, U.S.D.R.S. of 1910 (29 years).

1910-16:
$$X_1 = 4.5300 + .0890x$$
1919-40:
$$X_1 = 4.1400 - .1020x - .0080x^2 \quad (11)$$

30. Deaths by homicide, white, U.S.D.R.S. of 1910 (28 years).

1910-16:
$$X_1 = 4.5300 + .0890x$$
1919/1921-40:
$$X_1 = 4.0910 - .1110x - .0082x^2 \quad (13)[b]$$

31. Deaths by homicide, non-white, U.S.D.R.S. of 1910 (29 years).

1910-16:
$$X_1 = 24.4300 + .9820x$$
1919-40:
$$X_1 = 40.5080 - .2700x - .1320x^2 \quad (11)$$

32. Deaths by homicide, non-white, U.S.D.R.S. of 1910 (28 years)

1910-16:
$$X_1 = 24.4300 + .9820x$$
1919/1921-40:
$$X_1 = 40.2585 - .5161x - .1315x^2 \quad (13)[b]$$

Table 4—continued

33. Deaths by homicide, white, U.S.D.R.S. of 1920 (21 years).
1920-40:
$X_1 = 5.2470 - 1.0065x - .0132x^2$ (12)

34. Death by homicide, non-white, U.S.D.R.S. of 1920 (21 years).
1920-40:
$X_1 = 40.6688 + .0427x - .1030x^2$ (12)

35. Deaths by alcoholism, white, U.S.D.R.S. of 1900 (28 years).
1910-16:
$X_1 = 5.8430 + .1286x$
1919/1921-40:
$X_1 = 4.6640 - .0521x - .0269x^2$ (13)[b]

36. Deaths by alcoholism, non-white, U.S.D.R.S. of 1900 (28 years).
1910-16:
$X_1 = 7.5430 + .2640x$
1919/1921-40:
$X_1 = 9.8905 + .0949x - .0634x^2$ (13)[b]

37. Deaths by alcoholism, white, U.S.D.R.S. of 1910 (28 years).
1910-16:
$X_1 = 5.5430 + .0680x$
1919/1921-40:
$X_1 = 4.1619 - .0375x - .0222x^2$ (13)[b]

38. Deaths by alcoholism, non-white, U.S.D.R.S. of 1910 (28 years).
1910-16:
$X_1 = 6.8000 + .2714x$
1919/1921-40:
$X_1 = 9.2149 + .0209x - .0590x^2$ (13)[b]

39. Deaths by alcoholism, white, U.S.D.R.S. of 1920 (21 years).
1920-40:
$X_1 = 3.6749 - .0250x - .0211x^2$ (12)[b]

40. Deaths by alcoholism, non-white, U.S.D.R.S. of 1920 (21 years).
1920-40:
$X_1 = 4.7982 + .0570x - .0287x^2$ (12)[b]

41. Males admitted to state and federal prisons and reformatories for murder (16 years).
1926-41:
$X_1 = 3580.8609 + 40.7897x - 20.1787x^2$ (15 and 16)

42. Females admitted to state and federal prisons and reformatories for murder (16 years).
1926-41:
$X_1 = 291.8728 + 12.1162x - 1.0499x^2$ (15 and 16)

43. Burglary, 10 cities, large cycles (17 years).
1929-41/46-49:
$X_1 = 38,287.41 + 483.56x$ (1)

44. Burglary, 10 cities, small cycles (17 years).
1929-37:
$X_1 = 37,487.11 + 1201.18x$
1938-41/46-49:
$X_1 = 39,187.75 + 1523.79x$ (2)

45. Burglary, 10 cities, small cycles (13 years).
1929-41:
$X_1 = 36,840.31 + 183.47x$ (3)

46. Burglary, 55 cities, large cycles (16 years).
1930-41/46-49:
$X_1 = 50,121.97 + 656.79x + 133.95x^2$ (4)

47. Burglary, 55 cities, small cycles (16 years).
1930-37:
$X_1 = 51,178.25 + 17.83x$
1938-41/46-49:
$X_1 = 54,750.22 + 2571.13x + 1.6012x^2$ (5)

48. Burglary, 55 cities, small cycles (12 years).
1930-41:
$X_1 = 50,218.75 - 302.95x$ (6)

Table 4—continued

49. Burglary, Berkeley, small cycles (23 years).
1918/19-31/32:
$X_1 = 279.8390 + 9.4813x + .1154x^2$
1932/33-40/41:
$X_1 = 278.6666 + 8.9000x$ (14)

50. Burglary, Berkeley, small cycles (23 years).
1918/19-40-41:
$X_1 = 280.5217 + 2.4694x$ (14)

51. Burglary, Los Angeles, large cycles (17 years).
1925-41:
$X_1 = 8078.3520 + 109.8529x$ (8)

52. Burglary, Los Angeles, small cycles (17 years).
1925-33:
$X_1 = 7808.7778 + 170.1500x$
1934-41:
$X_1 = 8381.6250 + 333.0595x$ (7)

53. Burglary, Portland, large cycles (17 years).
1925-41:
$X_1 = 2300.0000 + 68.5539x$ (8)

54. Burglary, Portland, small cycles (17 years).
1925-41:
$X_1 = 2674.7672 + 63.5539x$
$- 15.6153x^2$ (7)

55. Burglary, Baltimore, small cycles (18 years).
1928-41/46-49:
$X_1 = 2189.0090 - 3.2900x$
$- 2.0024x^2$ (10)

56. Burglary, Rochester, large cycles (18 years).
1928-41/46-49:
$X_1 = 671.0000 + 2.9453x$ (9)

57. Burglary, Rochester, small cycles (18 years).
1928-37:
$X_1 = 694.6000 + 35.3818x$
1938-41/46-49:
$X_1 = 641.5000 + 15.0476x$ (10)

58. Robbery, 11 cities, large cycles (17 years).
1929-41/46-49:
$X_1 = 15,253.6847 - 458.9700x$
$+ 5.1700x^2$ (1)

59. Robbery, 11 cities, small cycles (17 years).
1929-37:
$X_1 = .17,534.6700 - 497.7000x$
1938-41/46-49:
$X_1 = 12,951.2500 + 181.0700x$ (2)

60. Robbery, 11 cities, small cycles (13 years).
1929-41:
$X_1 = 15,983.7700 - 675.0300x$ (3)

61. Robbery, Berkeley, small cycles (23 years).
1918/19-40/41:
$X_1 = 25.4348 - .4150x$ (14)

62. Robbery, Berkeley, small cycles (23 years).
1918/19-40/41:
$X_1 = 35.4052 - .4150x$
$- .2266x^2$ (14)

63. Robbery, Los Angeles, large cycles (17 years).
1925-41:
$X_1 = 1695.6290 + 19.7402x$
$- .3718x^2$ (8)

64. Robbery, Los Angeles, small cycles (17 years).
1925-33:
$X_1 = 1787.4444 + 147.8667x$
1934-41:
$X_1 = 1573.3750 + 164.0119x$ (7)

65. Robbery, Portland, large cycles (17 years).
1925-41:
$X_1 = 364.7059 + 1.5466x$ (8)

66. Robbery, Portland, small cycles. (17 years).
1925-32:
$X_1 = 364.0000 + 40.0000x$

Table 4—continued

1933-41:
$$X_1 = 315.9633 - 17.0833x$$
$$+ 7.4055x^2 \ (7)$$

67. Robbery, Baltimore, large cycles
(18 years).
1928-41/46-49:
$$X_1 = 515.7220 + 8.7049x \ (9)$$

68. Robbery, Boston, large cycles
(18 years).
1928-41/46-49:
$$X_1 = 334.1667 - 3.6047x \ (9)$$

69. Robbery, Boston, small cycles
(18 years).
1928-36:
$$X_1 = 353.1111 + 6.7559x$$
1937-41/46-49:
$$X_1 = 291.7156 - 10.2833x$$
$$+ 3.5260x^2 \ (10)$$

70. Robbery, Rochester, small cycles
(18 years).
1928-41/46-49:
$$X_1 = 35.6503 - 1.2539x$$
$$+ .1100x^2 \ (10)$$

a. Numbers in parentheses following equations refer to the business index from Table 3 of this Appendix with which each series is correlated.

b. These series are reported in Tables 5 and 6, Chapter III.

appendix III

▶ INTRODUCTION

Arthur F. Burns and Wesley C. Mitchell of the National Bureau of Economic Research have developed a technique for analyzing cycles in economic time series which provides more detailed information than the conventional method of time series correlation.[1]

Their technique was designed to determine (a) "what economic activities reveal recurrent sequences of expansion, recession, contraction, and revival, lasting more than one year but not more than ten or twelve years," (b) "how the specific cycles of different activities are related to one another in direction of movement, in timing of their peaks and troughs, and in the duration of their expansions and contractions;" and (c) the "amplitude of the cyclical movements of individual activities and of their rate of change during cyclical expansions and contractions."[2]

The technique yields information about relationships between series which correlation techniques fail to yield and is useful for the further understanding of the social aspects of business cycles. In earlier sections, we have used the technique to examine the relative sensitivity of social phenomena to expansion and recession of the business cycle and tendencies for correlated social data to lead or lag behind the business cycle.

In order that series which are expressed in different physical units may be comparable, original data are expressed as percentages of their average value during any given cycle. Cyclical patterns, and amplitudes and rates of change are then expressed in terms of these percentages as "relatives."

"Reference dates," i.e., dates of turning points of business cycles, were established by the authors for the United States, Great Britain, Germany and France. Annual, quarterly and monthly reference dates were determined for turning points of business cycles in each of these countries.[3] The authors use these reference dates as "benchmarks" for analysis of the relation of cyclical social and economic series with general business fluctuations.

The pattern of analysis has two parts.[4] One part is concerned with a description of the behavior of any given series in terms of its own cyclical movement. For this purpose, a series of specific cycle tables, or S-tables, are constructed. S-tables also contain data on leads or lags of specific cycle turning points with reference to corresponding reference cycle turning points. Following this, a similar group of tables is constructed, describing the behavior of the series under study during the reference or business cycles. These are called R-tables.

An economic or social series is broken into its "specific" cycles which are defined as the periodic fluctuations in amplitude typical of the series. Specific cycles are measured from peak to peak when the series under analysis is correlated negatively with the business cycle. Measurement of the number of months from initial peak to trough to terminal peak of each cycle gives the duration of expansion and contraction phases of each cycle. Cycle measures are averaged to produce a single average measure for all the cycles in the series.

Arithmetic means of the annual number of suicides during each cycle provide the bases on which "specific cycle relatives" are computed. A specific cyle relative is a percentage. Any value during the cycle can be converted into a relative by expressing it in terms of the mean number of suicides during the cycle. Amplitudes of the rise and fall of each specific cycle are expressed in cycle relatives. The cycle relatives, or "standings" at the peak, mid-contraction, trough, mid-expansion and terminal peak of each cycle, and their averages over all cycles in the series, are computed.

"Reference cycle relatives" are similarly computed by converting the values of the series during each reference or business cycle into percentages of their arithmetic mean. Reference cycle relatives at the troughs, peaks, mid-expansion and mid-contraction of the reference or business cycle show the pattern of behavior of the suicide series during various phases of the business cycle. Monthly rates of change between the five stages are computed.

A series of suicides of single persons in Cook County, Illinois, from 1906-1947, is analyzed by the Burns-Mitchell technique in the remainder of this Appendix to illustrate the fruitfulness of the method in revealing the nature of the relation between cyclical social and economic series. As is the case with most suicide series, only annual data are available for suicide of single persons in Cook County. The limitations of annual data in the technique have been stressed by Burns and Mitchell since annual data tend to distort or skip entirely a certain number of specific cycles. While its use limits the reliability of the analysis of timing and duration of specific cycles, it has the computational advantage of making the removal of seasonal trend unnecessary. The modifications suggested by the authors when annual data are used have been incorporated in the following illustration.

▶ SPECIFIC CYCLES

The series of suicide is broken into 11 specific cycles as shown in Table 1. Peaks of 8 of the specific cycles correspond with troughs of the "reference" or composite business cycles. Troughs of 8 of the suicide cycles correspond with peaks of the business cycle.[5] The expansion in business between 1911 and 1913 is not reflected in this suicide series and contractions in suicide between 1930 and 1931 and between 1937 and 1938 appear to be independent of business fluctuations.

When the war cycle from 1914 to 1919 is omitted, troughs of the suicide cycles precede their corresponding business peaks, on the average, by 5.6 months, while peaks of suicide cycles precede their corresponding business troughs by an average of 1.7 months. The expansion phase of the average suicide cycle lasts two years. The contraction phase averages only about 15 months.

Amplitude of Cycles of Suicide.—Rates of rise and fall of suicide during each cycle are computed, along with summary measures of the rates of increase and decrease averaged for all cycles in the series.

The number of suicides of single persons in Cook Country drops an average of 16 per cent from peak to trough. The most violent rate of fall, over 2 per cent per month, came between the suicide peak of 1937 and the trough of 1938. This rapid rate of fall occurred during a year when the business index also was falling from a peak in 1937 to a trough in 1938.

Secular Movements of Cycles of Suicide.—The Burns-Mitchell technique distinguishes the intra-cycle trend (that part of the secular movement which is observable within a single cycle), from the inter-cycle trend which is measured by the step-line formed by mean levels of successive cycles. The data show that a very slight downward secular trend of .06 per month characterizes the suicide series. The secular trend was rising during the decade of the twenties, a trend characteristic of many suicide series.

Patterns of Cycles of Suicide.—Specific cycle relatives at each of the 5 stages of a cycle of suicide are computed. Averages over all cycles are computed as usual. Peaks of the suicide cycles average about 7 per cent above the mean value of each specific cycle.[6] The mid-point of the contraction phase is nearly 2 per cent below the mean while the trough averages 9 per cent below the mean. The value at mid-expansion is .5 per cent below the mean and the terminal peak averages 12 per cent above the mean. Weighted averages, or arithmetic means of the rates of change in successive cycles weighted by the intervals to which the rates apply, were computed for our illustrative series.

The most violent weighted average monthly rate of fall (—1.28) occurs during the first half of the contraction phase of suicide cycles, between the peak and the mid-contraction. The average rate of rise is lowest (+.75) during the first half of expansion from the trough to the mid-point.

► REFERENCE CYCLES

Patterns of Reference Cycles.—Reference cycle patterns are similar to specific cycle patterns except that the "relatives" at each of the five stages are percentages of the average number of suicides during the reference or business cycle, rather than during the suicide cycle. Reference cycles are marked off by a set of reference dates corresponding to the turning points of business cycles. Table 2 presents the reference cycle pattern for the suicide series.

At the initial trough of business, suicide averages 2 per cent above the mean during the reference cycle. At the business peak it is 4 per cent below the mean. Our suicide series failed to reflect the depression trough of 1911 and the prosperity peak of 1913. At the business trough of 1914, suicide was 34 per cent above its mean for the war cycle.

This strong negative reaction of suicide to the depression of 1914 may be related to the outbreak of war, which reduced the average number of suicides during the cycle. At the peak of the

Table 1—Timing and Duration of Specific Cycles, Suicide of Single Persons, Cook County, Illinois, 1906-1947

DATES OF SPECIFIC CYCLES			TIMING AT REFERENCE PEAK		TIMING AT REFERENCE TROUGH	
			No. of Months Lead (—) or Lag (+)	Date of Reference Peak	No. of Months Lead (—) or Lag (+)	Date of Reference Trough
Peak	Trough (1)	Peak	(2)	(3)	(4)	(5)
1906	1907	1908	+ 1	May '07	0	June '08
1908	1909	1914	— 7	Jan. '10	— 6	Dec. '14
1914[a]	1918	1919	— 2	Aug. '18	+ 2	Apr. '19
1919	1920	1921	+ 5	Jan. '20	— 3	Sept. '21
1921	1923	1924	+ 1	May '23	— 1	July '24
1924	1925	1928	—16	Oct. '26	+ 6	Dec. '27
1928	1929	1930	0	June '29	..	......
1930	1931	1933	..	......	+ 3	Mar. '33
1933	1935	1937	—23	May '37	—11	May '38
1937	1938	1940	..	......	..	......
1940[a]	1944	1947	..	......	..	......
Total excluding war cycles			—39	......	—12	......
Average excluding war cycles			— 5.6	......	— 1.7	......
Average Deviation			8.4	......	4.2	......

a. War cycles.

business cycle running from 1932-1938, suicide was 5 per cent above its average for the period. At the business trough of 1938, suicide was 20 per cent below the mean for the cycle 1932-1938.

Rates of rise and fall of suicide during the phases of business cycles are computed in the same way as rates of change during suicide cycles. Table R-2 presenting the computations is omitted from this discussion. Suicide in weighted reference cycle relatives declines at an average rate of —.36 per cent per month during the first half of business expansion, continues to decline at a markedly lower rate of —.06 per cent during the last half, rises at the rate

Table 2—R1—Reference Cycle Patterns, Suicide of Single Persons, Cook County, Illinois, 1906-1947[a]

			AVERAGE IN REFERENCE CYCLE RELATIVES AT STAGE				
DATES OF REFERENCE CYCLES			I Initial Trough	III Mid-expansion	V Peak	VII Mid-contraction	IX Terminal Trough
Trough	Peak (1)	Trough	(2)	(4)	(6)	(8)	(10)
....	1907	1908	....	....	93.9	100.0	106.1
1908	1910	1911	107.9	92.5	101.8	102.2	102.5
1911	1913	1914	82.6	98.1	102.5	109.3	116.1
1914	1918	1919[b]	134.1	107.1	74.6	80.0	85.4
1919	1920	1921	105.3	96.0	86.7	104.4	122.1
1921	1923	1924	116.9	99.2	89.8	97.0	104.2
1924	1926	1927	101.7	94.2	97.5	105.0	112.4
1927	1929	1932	90.5	103.2	93.9	103.5	101.2
1932	1937	1938	110.8	97.3	105.0	92.9	80.9
Total excluding war			715.7	680.5	771.1	814.3	845.5
Average			102.2	97.2	96.4	101.8	105.7
Average Deviation			9.1	2.6	5.3	3.9	8.5

a. Average annual standings during each reference cycle on the basis of which reference cycle relatives are computed, are as follows:
1907-08 = 132.0; 1908-11 = 129.7; 1911-14 = 161.0; 1914-19 = 139.4; 1919-21 = 113.0; 1921-24 = 118.0; 1924-27 = 121.0; 1927-32 = 150.2; 1932-38 = 137.2.
b. War cycle.

of +.72 per cent during the first half of contraction, and continues to rise at a less rapid monthly rate (+.52 per cent) from mid-contraction to the terminal trough of business.

The sharpest average monthly rate of fall in suicide occurs in the first half of business expansion, and the sharpest average monthly rate of rise occurs in the first half of contraction. The excess in the monthly rate of fall during the first half of expansion over the second half is greater than the excess in the monthly rate of rise during the first half of contraction over the second half. Marked exceptions to this average pattern occur during the business cycles from 1911-1914, 1927-1932, and 1932-1938 and average deviations are large relative to the means.

If analysis of other suicide series confirms this finding that suicide rises and falls more rapidly immediately following the turning points of business than it does immediately prior to the turning points of business, the fruitfulness of the Burns-Mitchell technique for analysis of social data would be adequately demonstrated.

Conformity between Cycles of Business and Cycles of Suicide.— Burns and Mitchell measure the conformity of specific and reference cycles by the average change per month in reference cycle relatives during expansions and contractions. Our suicide series drops an average of .32 per cent per month during business expansions and rises .72 per cent per month during reference contractions.

An index of conformity to business expansions is computed by crediting the series with 100 for every rise in suicide during business expansion, debiting it with 100 for every fall, and writing 0 when there is no change. This expansion index for our series is —71.4. The contraction index computed in the same way is —.75. The negative signs indicate that suicide rises in business depression and falls during prosperity. The magnitudes indicate the degree of consistency in the direction of movement.

Figure 1 pictures the behavior of our suicide series during 7 business cycles between 1906-1947. The long horizontal line at the bottom of the chart represents the average duration of the 7 business or reference cycles. The horizontal line is broken by vertical lines erected at the two business troughs, the peaks, mid-expansion and mid-contraction. The troughs are marked "T" and the peaks "P." Length of these lines indicates average deviations of the reference cycle relatives. The vertical scale at the left runs in units of reference cycle relatives.

This Chart shows at a glance the average pattern of response of suicide to seven business cycles and graphically summarizes the important data of Tables 1 and 2.

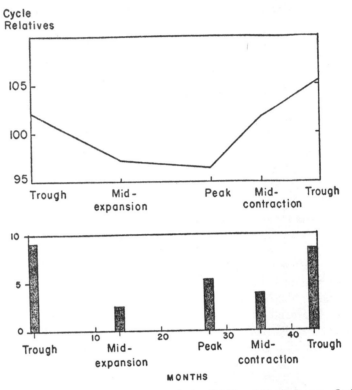

Figure 1. Pattern of Seven Reference Cycles, Suicide of Single Persons, Cook County, Illinois, 1906-1947. War Cycles Are Omitted.

▶ SUMMARY

We have presented this illustration of the Burns-Mitchell technique to point out its fruitfulness for the analysis of the relation between social data and economic forces. Its advantages over the technique of time series correlation are obvious. The technique may be applied to series of rates of marriage, divorce, fertility, mortality and other correlates of business cycles, as well as to futher series of suicide and homicide holding status constant. It will yield data on the way in which economic forces relate to social phenomena and insights into the stratification system of American society, derived from the differential effects of economic cycles on various status groupings within the population.

appendix IV

THE REACTION OF CYCLES OF

SUICIDE TO CYCLES OF BUSINESS

In this Appendix we are concerned with breaking down the negative relationship between cycles of suicide and cycles of business. The behavior of suicide at peaks and troughs of business cycles is examined together with rates of increase and decrease, and the differential sensitivity of suicide to business contractions and business expansions. This analysis rests heavily on the work of Mitchell and Burns of the National Bureau of Economic Research.[1] Two suicide series are analyzed in detail using this technique and certain summary measures are presented for 23 series of suicide of differing status categories in the United States.

▶ CORRESPONDENCE BETWEEN CYCLES OF SUICIDE AND
CYCLES OF BUSINESS

Reliable data about lapses of time in the response of suicide to cyclical changes in business would help us in explaining the high negative relation between business conditions and suicide.

In this section we will show how the turning points of suicide cycles match up with the corresponding turning points of business cycles. Because of the high negative correlation between suicide and business cycles, we should expect to find close correspondence between peaks of cycles of suicide and troughs of business cycles. Suicide should hit its peak in the same year that business cycles reach their troughs. Similarly, troughs of suicide should come in those years in which the business index is at a maximum. We will see, however, that in many cases, turning points of suicide cycles precede the turning points of business cycles with which they are matched.

Data.—Burns-Mitchell have described a technique for matching

Table 1—Behavior of Twenty-three Suicide Series at Business Troughs[a]

Suicide Series	NUMBER OF TIMES THE SUICIDE SERIES REACHES ITS PEAK				
	1-2 Years Before the Business Cycle Reaches Its Trough	The Same Year the Business Cycle Reaches Its Trough	1-2 Years After the Business Cycle Reaches Its Trough	Cases of Non-Correspondence at the Business Trough	Total
White[b]	0	5	1	1[f]	7
Non-white[b]	1	5	0	1[f]	7
Males[c]	0	6	2	1[f]	9
Females[c]	4	3	1	1[g]	9
White Males[d]	0	4	0	1[f]	5
White Females[d]	3	1	0	1[g]	5
Non-white Males[d]	0	4	0	1[f]	5
Non-white Females[d]	1	4	0	0	5
Males, 15-24[d]	1	4	0	0	5
Females, 15-24[d]	3	0	1	1[h]	5
Males, 25-34[d]	0	4	1	0	5
Females, 25-34[d]	2	2	1	0	5
Males, 35-44[d]	0	4	0	1[f]	5
Females, 35-44[d]	1	2	1	1[h]	5
Males, 45-54[d]	0	4	1	0	5
Females, 45-54[d]	3	0	0	2[gh]	5
Males, 55-64[d]	0	4	1	0	5
Females, 55-64[d]	3	1	0	1[g]	5
Males, 65-74[d]	0	2	1	2[fh]	5
Females, 65-74[d]	0	1	3	1[f]	5
Males, 75 and Over[d]	2	1	2	0	5
Single Persons[e]	1	4	2	1[i]	8
Married Persons[e]	1	4	2	1[i]	8
Males, Total	3	37	8	6	54
Females, Total	20	14	7	8	49
Total, 23 Series	26	69	20	18	133

a. Business troughs occurred in the years, 1904, 1908, 1911, 1914, 1921, 1924, 1927, 1932, and 1938.
  b. 1910-1941.
  c. 1900-1941.
  d. 1920-1941.
  e. 1905-1941.
  f. Non-correspondence at the 1927 trough.
  g. Non-correspondence at the 1921 trough.
  h. Non-correspondence at the 1924 trough.
  i. Non-correspondence at the 1911 trough.

"specific" or suicide cycles with "reference" or business cycles to see whether they "correspond."

Peaks of cycles of 23 different suicide time series were matched with the "reference" or business troughs to reveal any tendency for suicide peaks to occur either the same year as the corresponding business trough, a year or two before the business trough, or a year or two after the corresponding business trough. Table 1 summarizes the data from all 23 series.

Peaks of suicide tend to come during the same year as the troughs of business cycles with which they correspond. There is very little tendency for peaks of suicide either to precede or follow the corresponding troughs of business. Only 18 out of 133 peaks in the 23 suicide series fail to correspond to business troughs, using the matching criteria established by Burns-Mitchell.

When a series of suicide of males and females are considered separately, it becomes evident that peaks of suicide in the 10 male series occur the same year as business troughs with much greater frequency than the suicide peaks in the 9 female series. Peaks of female suicide precede their corresponding business troughs in 20 cases, and occur in the same year as the corresponding business troughs in only 14 cases. This is in sharp contrast to the correspondence pattern for male suicide, with suicide peaks occurring the same year as corresponding business troughs in about 70 per cent of the cases.

Eight of the 23 series failed to react to the business trough in 1927. Four of the series failed to respond to the 1921 business trough and four did not react to the 1924 trough.

We have described the tendency for peaks of suicide to come in the same years as troughs of business. The other half of the correspondence pattern—the matching of troughs of suicide with peaks of business—is shown in Table 2.

In sharp contrast with the pattern of correspondence of suicide peaks with business troughs, troughs of cycles of suicide tend to *precede* by a year or two the business peaks with which they are matched. There is no significant tendency for troughs of cycles of suicide to occur a year or two after the corresponding business peak.

While the tendency for troughs of cycles of suicide to precede peaks of business cycles is more marked for females than for males, troughs of male suicide occur in the same years as the corresponding business peaks about as often as they precede business peaks. Eight of the 23 suicide series failed to react to the business peak of 1929.

Table 3 summarizes the behavior of suicide at the turning points of business cycles, omitting cases of non-correspondence and cases

Table 2—Behavior of Twenty-three Suicide Series at Business Peaks[a]

Suicide Series	NUMBER OF TIMES THE SUICIDE SERIES REACHES ITS TROUGH				
	1-2 Years Before the Business Cycle Reaches Its Peak	The Same Year the Business Cycle Reaches Its Peak	1-2 Years After the Business Cycle Reaches Its Peak	Cases of Non-Corre-spondence at the Business Peak	Total
White, U.S.[b]	2	3	0	1[f]	6
Non-White, U.S.[b]	2	3	0	1[f]	6
Males, U.S.[c]	4	4	0	1[f]	9
Females, U.S.[c]	3	3	1	2[g,h]	9
White Males[d]	2	1	0	1[f]	4
White Females[d]	3	0	0	1[i]	4
Non-White Males[d]	2	1	0	1[f]	4
Non-White Females[d]	2	2	0	0	4
Males, 15-24[d]	2	1	1	0	4
Females, 15-24[d]	2	1	0	1[i]	4
Males, 25-34[d]	1	3	0	0	4
Females, 25-34[d]	3	0	1	0	4
Males, 35-44[d]	2	1	0	1[f]	4
Females, 35-44[d]	2	1	0	1[g]	4
Males, 45-54[d]	2	2	0	0	4
Females, 45-54[d]	3	0	0	1[i]	4
Males, 55-64[d]	2	2	0	0	4
Females, 55-64[d]	3	0	0	1[i]	4
Males, 65-74[d]	0	2	0	2[f,g]	4
Females, 65-74[d]	0	2	1	1[f]	4
Males, 75 and Over[d]	3	1	0	0	4
Single Persons[e]	3	4	0	1[j]	8
Married Persons[e]	2	5	0	1[j]	8
Males, Total	20	18	1	6	45
Females, Total	21	9	3	8	41
Total, 23 Series	50	42	4	18	114

a. Business peaks occurred in the years 1903, 1907, 1910, 1913, 1920, 1923, 1926, 1929, and 1937.
b. 1910-1941.
c. 1900-1941.
d. 1920-1941.
e. 1905-1941.
f. Non-correspondence at the 1929 peak.
g. Non-correspondence at the 1926 peak.
h. Non-correspondence at the 1937 peak.
i. Non-correspondence at the 1923 peak.
j. Non-correspondence at the 1913 peak.

Table 3—Correspondence of Turning Points of Suicide and Business Cycles*

	AT BUSINESS PEAKS		AT BUSINESS TROUGHS	
By Sex and Total	Per Cent of Suicide Troughs Occurring a Year or Two Earlier	Per Cent of Suicide Troughs Occurring the Same Year	Per Cent of Suicide Peaks Occurring a Year or Two Earlier	Per Cent of Suicide Peaks Occurring the Same Year
Males	.53	.47	.08	.92
Females	.70	.30	.59	.41
Total	.54	.46	.27	.73

* Data from Tables 1 and 2. Cases where the suicide turning point follows the business turning point, and cases of non-correspondence, are omitted from this summary table.

where the suicide turning point follows the business cycle turning point.

The tendency for troughs of suicide cycles to precede peaks of business cycles with which they correspond is stronger than the tendency for peaks of suicide cycles to precede troughs of business cycles. The tendency for turning points of cycles of female suicide to precede the corresponding business cycle turning points is stronger than the tendency for turning points of cycles of male suicide to precede their corresponding business cycle turning points. This differential tendency is particularly marked at business troughs.

The business cycle most frequently "skipped" by suicide series was the one with a trough in 1927 and a peak in 1929. Eight series of suicide failed to react to the 1927-1929 business cycle in the expected negative direction.

▶ DIFFERENTIAL SENSITIVITY OF SUICIDE SERIES TO PERIODS OF
BUSINESS CONTRACTION AND BUSINESS EXPANSION

In this section we are concerned with the behavior of the suicide rate during "reference" or business cycles, as marked off by "reference dates" reflecting turning points of business cycles in the United States. The "reference cycle" concept, as formulated by Burns-Mitchell, makes it possible to separate out the response of suicide during business contractions and during business expansions. The technique yields a "reference cycle pattern" and provides information on the rates of change of suicide during various phases of business cycles.

Data.—The average reference cycle patterns for the two series of suicide receiving detailed treatment are presented in Table 4. The average suicide rate during a reference cycle (the time period between two successive troughs of business) serves as the base for the computation of reference cycle relatives.

Table 4—Average Reference Cycle Pattern, Two Series

Suicide Series	Initial Trough	AVERAGE IN REFERENCE CYCLE RELATIVES Mid-expansion	Peak	Mid-con-traction	Terminal Trough
Males, (8 cycles)	100.9	96.7	97.0	103.4	108.8
Females, (8 cycles)	99.4	98.2	100.3	102.4	103.8

Differences in reference cycle relatives between adjacent "stages" of reference cycles, corrected for the average annual time span between stages, makes it possible to compute annual rates of change in the suicide rate between the stages. These rates of change for our two series of suicide are presented in Tables 5 and 6.

Table 5 shows clearly the greater sensitivity of suicide to periods of contraction in business as compared with periods of expansion. For both series, the average annual rate of rise in suicide during contraction phases in business cycles is about four times as great as the average annual rate of fall in suicide during expansion phases.

Table 5—Average Annual Rate of Change in Reference Cycle Relatives for Two Series

Suicide Series	Average Rate of Fall in Suicide During Expansion Phases of the Business Cycle	Average Rate of Rise in Suicide During Contraction Phases of the Business Cycle
Male	−2.3	+9.5
Female	−0.5	+2.9

The Burns-Mitchell analysis makes possible a further breakdown of the "rate of change" pattern during phases of business cycles. Table 6 presents the average annual rates of change in the two suicide series during both halves of the reference expansion and both halves of the reference contraction.

For both of the series, the rate of fall of suicide is sharper during

Table 6—Average Annual Rate of Change from Stage to Stage, in Reference Cycle Relatives: Two Series

Suicide Series	AVERAGE ANNUAL RATE OF CHANGE IN REFERENCE CYCLE RELATIVES			
	DURING PERIOD OF BUSINESS EXPANSION		DURING PERIOD OF BUSINESS CONTRACTION	
	First Half	Second Half	First Half	Second Half
Males	−3.5	+0.3	+10.6	+0.1
Females	−1.0	+1.8	+ 3.5	+2.4

the first half of the business expansion than during the latter half (the half immediately preceding the business peak). In fact, the suicide rate is rising along with the business index just prior to the business peak. The rate of rise of suicide immediately following the business peak is also somewhat greater than the rate of rise during the final half of the business contraction. In both of the series, the suicide rate is rising during the final half of the average business expansion.

One of the weaknesses of the correlation technique is its inability to distinguish the differential sensitivity of suicide to business expansions as compared with business contractions. A simple way of getting this information is to add up, for our 23 suicide time series, the number of years the suicide rate is rising while the business index is falling, and the number of years the suicide rate is falling while the business index is rising.

Ayres' Index of Industrial Activity was rising during 27 and falling during 11 of the 38 peace-time years between 1900 and 1941. Table 7 presents, for each of the 23 series, the direction of movement of the suicide rate during the years in which the business index was rising. Table 8 presents, for the same 23 series, the direction of movement of suicide during the years in which the business index was falling.

In 209 of the 376 cases of business expansion (about 56 per cent), the suicide rate was falling. When the 10 males series and the 9 female series are treated separately, 62 per cent of the male cases responded negatively (by falling during periods of business expansion), while only 44 per cent of the female cases responded negatively. Suicide of females responded positively to increases in the business index (by rising during the years in which the business

Table 7—Behavior of Twenty-three Suicide Series during Years in Which the Business Index Was Rising[a]

NUMBER OF YEARS IN WHICH THE SUICIDE RATE

Suicide Series	Was Falling	Remained Constant	Was Rising	Total
White, U.S.[b]	11	2	6	19
Non-White, U.S.[b]	13	0	6	19
Males, U.S.[c]	17	1	9	27
Females, U.S.[c]	12	5	10	27
White Males[d]	8	1	5	14
White Females[d]	4	1	9	14
Non-White Males[d]	9	0	5	14
Non-White Females[d]	9	0	5	14
Males, 15-24[d]	9	0	5	14
Females, 15-24[d]	6	4	4	14
Males, 25-34[d]	8	2	4	14
Females, 25-34[d]	5	1	8	14
Males, 35-44[d]	8	0	6	14
Females, 35-44[d]	7	0	7	14
Males, 45-54[d]	11	0	3	14
Females, 45-54[d]	6	0	8	14
Males, 55-64[d]	10	0	4	14
Females, 55-64[d]	8	0	6	14
Males, 65-74[d]	9	0	5	14
Females, 65-74[d]	4	0	10	14
Males, 75 and Over[d]	6	0	8	14
Single Persons[e]	12	0	11	23
Married Persons[e]	17	0	6	23
Males, Total	95	4	54	153
Females, Total	61	11	67	139
Total, 23 Series	209	17	150	376

a. The business index was rising during the following years: 1900-1903, 1904-1907, 1908-1910, 1911-1913, 1914-1916, 1919-1920, 1921-1923, 1924-1926, 1927-1929, 1932-1937, 1938-1941.
b. 1910-1941, excluding war years.
c. 1900-1941, excluding war years.
d. 1920-1941, excluding war years.
e. 1905-1941, excluding war years.

index was rising), more often than it responded negatively.

In 6 of the 7 cases of comparison of male-female suicide response to business expansions, the pattern of a stronger negative response of the male series holds up. The single exception is the case of non-white males and non-white females, where sex appears to make no difference in the degree of negative response to business expansion. The negative correspondence of suicide to contractions in business is much stronger than the negative correspondence of suicide to expansions in business, as seen from Table 8. In 141 of the 179 cases of business contraction (nearly 80 per cent), the suicide rate was rising. The negative reaction of suicide of males to business contractions is much stronger than the negative reaction of female suicide. While 93 per cent of the cases of male suicide reacted negatively to business contractions, only about 57 per cent of the cases of female suicide reacted negatively. The only two female series reacting in a strong negative direction to business contractions were the non-white female series and females aged 65-74.

Negative reaction of suicide to business contractions is stronger than negative reaction of suicide to business expansions. Negative reaction of suicide of males to both business expansions and business contractions is stronger than negative reaction of suicide of females to both business expansions and business contractions.

Eleven of the 23 suicide series failed to react negatively to the 22 per cent fall in the business index between 1937 and 1938. Eight of the series did not respond negatively to the business decline between 1923-1924, and six of the series failed to react negatively to the business drop between 1931-1932. All of the 23 series responded negatively to the 19 per cent decline in the business index between 1929-1930, immediately following the 1929 peak.

Discussion.—Analysis of our two series by the Burns-Mitchell technique reveals marked differentials in the annual rates of change of suicide during business expansions and business contractions. Average annual rates of rise of suicide during business contractions are about four times as great as average annual rates of fall of suicide during business expansions. Analysis of our 23 suicide series confirms the finding that the negative reaction of the suicide rate to business contractions is stronger than the negative reaction of suicide to business expansions. This differential reaction is stronger for suicide of males than for suicide of females.

While annual rates of increase in suicide during periods of depression are greater than annual rates of decrease of suicide during periods of prosperity, rates of increase of suicide also are somewhat higher during the first half of the business contraction (the half immediately following the business peak) than during the final or pre-trough half of the business contraction.

Data presented in Table 6 show a pattern consistent for our two series. Rates of fall during business expansions are greater during

Table 8—Behavior of Twenty-three Suicide Series during Years in Which the Business Index Was Falling[a]

NUMBER OF YEARS IN WHICH THE SUICIDE RATE

Suicide Series	Was Rising	Remained Constant	Was Falling	Total
White, U.S.[b]	9	0	0	9
Non-White, U.S.[b]	8	1	0	9
Males, U.S.[b]	11	0	0	11
Females, U.S.[c]	6	3	2	11
White Males[d]	7	0	0	7
White Females[d]	3	0	4	7
Non-white Males[d]	7	0	0	7
Non-white Females[d]	6	0	1	7
Males, 15-24[d]	5	1	1	7
Females, 15-24[d]	3	0	4	7
Males, 25-34[d]	7	0	0	7
Females, 25-34[d]	4	0	3	7
Males, 35-44[d]	7	0	0	7
Females, 35-44[d]	4	1	2	7
Males, 45-54[d]	7	0	0	7
Females, 45-54[d]	2	0	5	7
Males, 55-64[d]	7	0	0	7
Females, 55-64[d]	4	0	3	7
Males, 65-74[d]	6	1	0	7
Females, 65-74[d]	6	0	1	7
Males, 75 & Over[d]	5	0	2	7
Single Persons[e]	8	0	2	10
Married Persons[e]	9	0	1	10
Male, Total	69	2	3	74
Female, Total	38	4	25	67
Total, 23 Series	141	7	31	179

a. The business index was falling during the following years: 1903-1904, 1907-1908, 1910-1911, 1913-1914, 1920-1921, 1923-1924, 1926-1927, 1929-1932, 1937-1938.
b. 1910-1941, excluding war years.
c. 1900-1941, excluding war years.
d. 1920-1941, excluding war years.
e. 1905-1941, excluding war years.

the first half of the expansion immediately following the business trough than during the second half of business expansion—the half immediately preceding the business peak. In both series, the suicide rate actually is rising along with the business index during the final pre-peak half of business expansion.

During the initial phase of recovery in business following the depth of the depression, suicide responds by beginning to decrease. But as the business recovery gets under way and prosperity nears its peak, suicide responds by ending its decline and beginning to rise. This type of reaction accounts for the positive relation found for many series between the suicide rate and expansions in business.

Our data indicate, despite the high negative correlations between suicide and the business cycle, that expansions in business, in about half of our cases, bring with them expansions in suicide rates. Further, this tendency for a positive association during business expansions is concentrated at the final pre-peak stage of business expansion.

When we hold constant the percentage increase in Ayres' business index during years of business expansion, we find that suicide falls with greater frequency during years of sharp increase in business than during years of small increase in business. When the percentage increase in the business index during the year is high, rates of suicide for the majority of our series decrease. When the percentage increase in the business index is low, rates of suicide for the majority of our series increase. But suicide rates do show a tendency to rise during final pre-peak phases of expansion in business cycles, and troughs of about half of our cycles of suicide do precede in time the peaks of business cycles with which they are matched.

► BURGLARY

Offenses of violence against property in the United States show persistent relationships with the economic cycle.[1] A time series of the number of burglaries known to the police in ten cities was correlated with Ayres' business index. These ten cities were selected because data on crimes known to the police were available for them since 1929, one year before the uniform crime reporting system began.[2]

A straight line trend fitted to the burglary index cuts off the large cyclical movement of the series but does not isolate the small fluctuations in the series between 1936 and 1941. When the fluctuations about this large cycle trend are expressed in terms of standard deviations, they may be compared graphically with the fluctuations about the trend in the business index. This is illustrated in Figure 1(A).[3] There is an inverse relation between the two variables but the degree of the relationship is difficult to determine. The fluctuations early in both series are large and their relationship is clearly negative. After 1935, however, the two series fluctuate positively. The two series correlate —.46.

We may cut off the small fluctuation in burglary between 1937 and 1938 which corresponds to the small cycle fluctuation of busi-

174

ness during the same period. Two trend lines have been used to isolate this fluctuation.

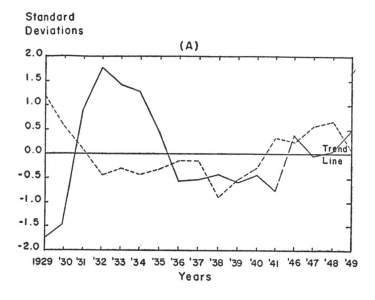

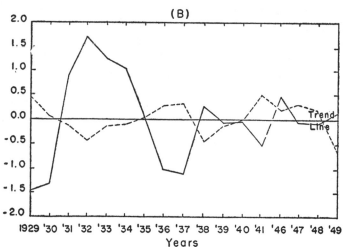

Figure 1. Large (A) and Small (B) Cycles of Burglary (—) and the Business Cycle (— —), Expressed in Terms of Standard Deviations of Each Series, 1929-41/46-49.

By fitting a straight line to this series during the years, 1929-37, and another straight line from 1938-41/46-49, the 1937-38 fluctuation is isolated. In so doing, we are to some extent removing the effect of the rapid rise in burglaries which occurred during the war, and possibly mitigating the influence of the large volume of depression-administered relief upon burglaries.[4] The existence of the war-time rise complicates the relation between the business cycle and burglary in that it probably is not due to influences of business conditions. By fitting the two straight line trends we may be, in effect, removing the distorting influence of the war years. The second straight line cuts the post war years in a manner similar to a straight line trend fitted to the four post-war years alone.

When the small cycle fluctuations of burglary and the business cycle are compared in Figure 1(B), the correspondence is markedly greater than in the case of large cycles. In 13 out of 17 years in the series, burglary and the business cycle fluctuate inversely. In the remaining years, fluctuations are small and so do not greatly detract from the inverse relationship of the series. The coefficient of correlation obtained for these data (—.64) is higher than that for large cycles of burglary and the business cycle.

A check on the small cycle analysis is obtained by correlating burglary with the business cycle for the shorter period, 1929-41. In this manner the war is more completely eliminated as an influence on the relation under study. By fitting a single straight line to the burglary series and correlating the fluctuations so isolated with fluctuations of the business cycle for this period, a coefficient of —.74 is obtained.

As a further check on the foregoing analysis, we investigated a second burglary index for 55 cities, 1930-41/46-49.[5] The large cycle trend fitted to this index is a second degree parabola. The correlation of large cycles of this series with large cycles of business for the same period is very low (—.11). The fact that 1929, a business cycle peak, is not included in this series may be important in this low correlation, though the most important factor would seem to be the smaller rise in burglaries between 1930-32 in our second index.

Small cycles in the 1930-41/46-49 burglary series are isolated by the same technique as was applied to the 1929 series. The coefficient of correlation obtained for small cycle analysis is —.37. The small cycle analysis is checked by comparing the 1930 series of burglaries with the business cycle for the pre-war years from 1930-41. The fluctuations isolated by fitting a straight line to both the business cycle and burglary for this period correlated —.44. This is the highest coefficient of correlation obtained between the 1930 series of burglary and the business cycle.

► ROBBERY

Robberies experience a spectacular rise between 1929 and 1932 after which they fall rapidly to a trough in 1936.[6] In 1936 robberies fall to a point below the index in 1929. The series is relatively stable between 1936 and 1941. Robberies increase less than 10 per cent between 1941 and 1946 in contrast to the more than 25 per cent rise experienced by the 10 cities burglary index.

When a second degree parabola is fitted to this series, the large cycle is isolated but the small fluctuations between 1936-37-38 is not. The fact that this curve places all the post-war years except 1946 above the trend lowers the correlation with the business cycle. This can be seen graphically by comparing the fluctuations of the robbery and business cycle indexes when they are expressed in terms of standard deviations of each series.

As illustrated in Figure 2(A), early in the series the fluctuations of both robbery and the business cycle tend to be large and inversely related. After 1934, the negative relationship ends. Viewing the series as a whole, in only 7 of the 17 years is the relation of the two series negative. But fluctuations for these 7 years are large enough to make the correlation for the entire series negative. The coefficient of correlation between the series is —.38.

In isolating small cycles of robbery, it is necessary to use two trend lines. The small fluctuation between 1936-41 is revealed when straight lines are fitted to the years 1929-37 and 1938-41/46-49.

The small cycle fluctuations of robbery, Figure 2(B), indicate a close relation between the variables. In all but one year, the fluctuations are inversely related. This fact is reflected in the coefficient of —.65 between the series.

Standard
Deviations

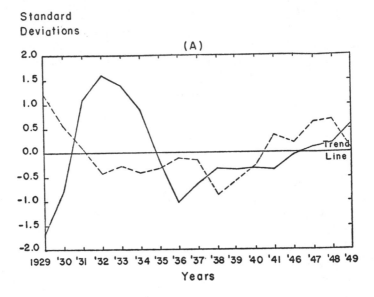

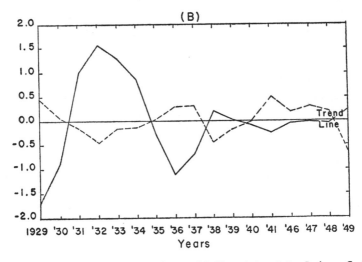

Figure 2. Large (A) and Small (B) Cycles of Robbery (—) and the Business Cycle
(— —), Expressed in Terms of Standard Deviations of Each Series, 1929-41/46-49.

► SUMMARY

The correlations obtained between selected cities' indexes of both burglary and robbery and the business cycle are presented in tabular form in Table 1.

Table 1—Correlations between the Business Cycle and Crimes of Violence Against Property in Selected Cities for Specified Periods, by Large and Small Cycles

Index	Large Cycle Correlation	Small Cycle Correlation
Burglaries, 1929-41/46-49[a]	—.46	—.64
Burglaries, 1930-41/46-49[b]	—.11	—.37
Burglaries, 1929-41[a]	. . . .	—.74
Burglaries, 1930-41[b]	. . . .	—.44
Robberies, 1929-41/46-49[c]	—.38	—.65
Robberies, 1929-41[c]	. . . .	—.65

a. Correlations for these periods are for the following cities: Baltimore, Chicago, Cincinnati, Cleveland, Denver, Detroit, Kansas City (Kansas), Los Angeles, Rochester (N. Y.), and Wichita.
b. Correlations for these periods are for the 55 cities listed in footnote b, Table 1, Chapter III, with the exceptions that Newark (N. J.), and San Francisco are not included and Lowell (Mass.) and Richmond (Va.) are included in this index.
c. Correlations for these periods are for the following cities: Baltimore, Boston, Chicago, Cincinnati, Cleveland, Denver, Detroit, Kansas City (Kansas), Los Angeles, Rochester (N. Y.), and Wichita.

In summary, we note the consistently negative coefficients of correlation between crimes of violence against property and the business cycle. We note also that small cycle correlations are consistently higher for the same indexes than are large cycle correlations.

With the limitations of data for individual cities in mind, we have analyzed burglary and robbery series for a number of large cities for which "crimes known to the police" data are available prior to 1929. Table 2 summarizes this analysis. Data for individual cities strongly support the conclusion of a negative relation between crimes of burglary and robbery with the business cycle. This is particularly significant in view of the differing time periods, the sections of the country represented, and the variation in city size.

It is not legitimate to interpret the differences in the magnitude of the coefficients. But the general consistency of the pattern of negative correlations does permit the conclusion of a strong and persistent tendency for robberies and burglaries to fall in prosperity and rise during depression.

Tables 3 and 4 show the sensitivity of the burglary and robbery

Table 2—Correlations between the Business Cycle and Crimes Against Property with Violence Known to the Police in Individual Cities for Specified Periods by Large and Small Cycles

City	Period	Large Cycle Correlation	Small Cycle Correlation
		BURGLARY	
Berkeley, Calif.	1919-41[a]	....	−.20
Los Angeles	1925-41[b]	....	−.78[c]
Portland, Oregon	1925-41[b]	....	−.71[d]
Baltimore	1928-41/46-49	....	−.42
Rochester, N. Y.	1928-41/46-49	−.59	−.67
		ROBBERY	
Berkeley, Calif.	1919-41[a]	....	−.26
Los Angeles	1925-41[b]	....	−.72[e]
Portland, Oregon	1925-41[b]	....	−.36[f]
Baltimore	1928-41/46-49	−.70	−.25
Boston	1928-41/46-49	−.59	−.55
Rochester, N. Y.	1928-41/46-49	....	−.58

a. Berkeley data are for the fiscal period July 1 through June 30 of the years specified. These data are not available after 1941 for our purposes because the Berkeley Police Department changed over to calendar year reports in 1945.

b. Post-war data for Los Angeles and Portland have not been included in this analysis. Crimes in these cities experienced exceptionally large rises between 1941 and 1946, due in large part to the influx of population into these areas during and following the war.

c. This correlation is obtained when a second degree parabola is fitted to the burglary series. When a straight line trend is fitted to this series, the correlation becomes −.20.

d. This correlation is obtained when a second degree parabola is fitted to the burglary series. When a straight line trend is fitted to this series, the correlation becomes −.80.

e. This correlation is obtained when a second degree parabola is fitted to the robbery series. When a straight line trend is fitted to this series, the correlation becomes −.19.

f. This correlation is obtained when a second degree parabola is fitted to the robbery series. When a straight line trend is fitted to this series, the correlation becomes −.53.

indexes employed in Table 1 of this appendix to changes in the business index during periods of business prosperity and depression. When the business index is falling (Table 3) robberies and burglaries increase during all three of the phases. But when the index is rising during periods of prosperity (Table 4) burglaries

Table 3—Behavior of Violent Crimes Against Property during Years in Which the Business Index Was Falling

Phase of the Business Cycle	NUMBER OF YEARS IN WHICH THE INCIDENCE OF CRIME	
	Was Falling	Was Rising
Prosperity[c]	0	3
Transition[b]	1	8
Depression[c]	0	2
Total	1	13

a. Business index is above the long term trend during periods of "prosperity."
b. Movements in the business index which cross the long term trend line.
c. Business index is below the long term trend during periods of "depression."

and robberies are also rising. During the transitional and depression phases of the cycle, these crimes drop off during years in which the business index is rising.

Most writers agree with Radzinowicz that these crimes are "mostly committed by those classes of society which normally border on the poverty line."[7] As economic conditions take a turn for the worse, the deprivation suffered by these marginal groups is reflected in an increase in crimes against property.

Table 4—Behavior of Violent Crimes Against Property during Years In Which the Business Index Was Rising

Phase of the Business Cycle*	NUMBER OF YEARS IN WHICH THE INCIDENCE OF CRIME	
	Was Rising	Was Falling
Prosperity	7	2
Transition	0	6
Depression	3	15
Total	10	23

* See preceding Table for definition of phases of the business cycle.

But after recovery from depression is well under way during the final stages of prosperity, burglaries and robberies stop their decrease and begin to rise again.

The few cases available require caution in an attempt to rationalize these findings. But if further research should sustain the finding that violent crimes against property increase during the final stages of business prosperity prior to the business peak, the explanation may lie in frustrations imposed on marginal economic groups who "lose" status relative to higher status categories during expansion phases of business cycles.[8] The general tendency for these crimes to rise in depression and fall in prosperity is clear. Violent crimes against property bear a radically different relation with the business cycle than violent crimes against persons.

▶ CHAPTER I

1. Emile Durkheim, *Suicide*, trans. John A. Spaulding and George Simpson (Glencoe, Illinois: The Free Press, 1951), pp. 152-160.
2. *Ibid.*, pp. 250-254.
3. *Ibid.*, p. 254.
4. Max Weber, *The Theory of Social and Economic Organization*, trans. A. M. Henderson and Talcott Parsons (New York: Oxford University Press, 1947).
5. Ruth S. Cavan, *Suicide* (Chicago: University of Chicago Press, 1928).
6. Durkheim, *op. cit.*, pp. 257-259.
7. Weber, *op. cit.*, p. 168.

▶ CHAPTER II

1. Talcott Parsons, "An Analytical Approach to the Theory of Social Stratification," *Essays In Sociological Theory, Pure and Applied* (Glencoe, Illinois: The Free Press, 1949), pp. 166-84.
2. *Ibid.*, p. 171.
3. *Ibid.*, p. 171.
4. *Ibid.*, p. 172.
5. "American Business Activity Since 1790" (23rd ed.; Cleveland, Ohio: The Cleveland Trust Company, 1950), p. 1.
6. Percentage based on 172 cases. See App. IV, Table 8.
7. Percentage based on 359 cases. See App. IV, Table 7.
8. See App. IV, Table 1. App. III illustrates the Burns-Mitchell technique in greater detail.
9. Cases where the suicide trough either failed to correspond with the business peak, or followed it in time are excluded. See App. IV, Table 2.
10. See App. IV, Table 5.

11. See App. IV, Table 6.

12. Emile Durkheim, *Suicide,* trans. John A. Spaulding and George Simpson (Glencoe, Illinois: The Free Press, 1951), p. 253.

13. See Talcott Parsons and Edward A. Shils, *Toward A General Theory of Action* (Cambridge: Harvard University Press, 1951), for a discussion of systems of value orientation.

14. See App. II for a discussion of the correlation technique as applied here.

15. The war years, 1917-1918 and 1942-1946 were excluded from all correlations.

16. Louis I. Dublin and Bessie Bunzel, *To Be or Not To Be* (New York: Harrison Smith and Robert Haas, 1933), p. 104.

17. For a discussion of the historical development of the Negro family in America, see E. Franklin Frazier, *The Negro Family in the United States* (Chicago: University of Chicago Press, 1939), pp. 89-162.

18. See App. II, Table 4, No. 25.

19. See App. II, Table 4, No. 26.

20. Cities with a population of 10,000 or more.

21. Rural areas include cities with a population of less than 10,000.

22. Myrdal has noted the parallel between the lower status of white females as compared with white males, and the lower status of Negroes as compared with whites. Historically, females have been surpressed by males in much the same manner in which Negroes have been supressed by whites. See Gunnar Myrdal, *An American Dilemma* (New York: Harper and Brothers, 1944), pp. 1073-78.

23. Talcott Parsons, "Age and Sex in the Social Structure of the United States," *American Sociological Review,* VII (October, 1942), pp. 604-16.

24. *Ibid.,* p. 608.

25. Ruth S. Cavan, *et al. Personal Adjustment in Old Age* (Chicago: Science Research Associates, 1949).

26. See App. II, Table 2, No. 27.

27. See App. II, Table 2, No. 28.

28. Robert Cooley Angell, *The Family Encounters the Depression* (New York: Charles Scribner's Sons, 1936).

29. Ruth Shonle Cavan and Katherine Howland Ranck, *The Family and the Depression* (Chicago: University of Chicago Press, 1938).

30. Mirra Komarovsky, *The Unemployed Man and His Family* (New York: The Dryden Press, Inc., 1940).

31. The problem is, of course, further complicated by the interdependent relationships of the three variables of age, marital status and sex with the rate of unemployment during periods of depression. For a comprehensive statement of the "research problem" in untangling the inter-relationships among these variables, see Samuel A. Stouffer and Paul F. Lazarsfeld, *Research Memorandum on the Family in the De-*

pression (New York: Social Science Research Council, Bulletin No. 29, 1937), pp. 28-48.

32. "American Business Activity Since 1790," *op. cit.*, p. 1.

33. Andrew F. Henry, "The Nature of the Relation Between Suicide and the Business Cycle" (Unpublished Ph.D. dissertation, Dept. of Sociology, University of Chicago, 1950). Data from Louis Wirth and Margaret Furez (eds.), *Local Community Fact Book, 1938,* A Report Prepared for the Chicago Recreation Commission (Chicago: Chicago Recreation Commission, 1938). See also Louis Wirth and Eleanor Bernert (eds.), *Local Community Fact Book of Chicago* (Chicago: University of Chicago Press, 1949).

34. Median rental in the 16 high rent community areas varies between $42 and $79 a month. These 16 community areas had a population of 777,546 in 1930 and 811,405 in 1940. There were 121 suicides per year between 1930-1932 and 91 per year between 1939-1941. The "depression" suicide rate for these high rental areas was 15.5 per 100,000, while the "prosperity" or 1939-1941 rate for the same areas was 11.3 per 100,000.

35. Median rental in the 16 low rent community areas varies between $12 and $33 per month. The low rent areas had a combined population of 740,162 in 1930 and 655,576 in 1940. There were 138 suicides per year between 1930-1932 and 100 per year between 1939-1941. The "depression" or 1930-1932 rate for these low rental areas was 18.6 per 100,000 while the "prosperity" or 1939-1941 rate for the same areas was 15.3 per 100,000.

36. The 14 high rent areas with 100 per cent white populations had a "depression" suicide rate of 15.9 and a "prosperity" rate of 11.3. The 13 low rent all white areas had a "depression" rate of 16.3 and a "prosperity" rate of 15.3.

37. For a critique of ecological correlations, see W. S. Robinson, "Ecological Correlations and the Behavior of Individuals," *American Sociological Review,* XV (June, 1950), pp. 351-57.

► CHAPTER III

1. See Appendix V for demonstration of the existence of a negative correlation between crimes of violence against property and the business cycle. While the relation of homicide with the business cycle is positive, the relation of burglary and robbery is consistently negative.

2. The distinction between large and small cycles of business and social phenomena is elaborated in Appendix II. For the rationale of the selection of crimes indexes and a discussion of the reliability of the data, see James F. Short, Jr., "An Investigation of the Relation Between Crime and Business Cycles," (Unpublished Ph.D. dissertation, Department of Sociology, University of Chicago, 1951), chap. ii.

3. Only the eight *groups* of cities reported in Table 1 of this Chapter are included in the analysis presented in Tables 2 and 3.

4. Dorothy S. Thomas, *Social Aspects of the Business Cycle* (New York: Alfred A. Knopf, 1927), p. 144.

5. L. Radzinowicz, "The Influence of Economic Conditions on Crime," *Sociological Review*, XXXIII (July and October, 1941), p. 150.

6. During a part of this period, prohibition was in force. While few would argue that the consumption of alcohol experienced any marked change, variation in the cost of bootleg liquor might affect somewhat the correlation between deaths by alcoholism and the business cycle. It would require extensive research to determine the effect of the "noble experiment" on these relationships. Our working assumption is that the effect, if any, was very slight.

7. Erwin L. Linn, "The Correlation of Death Rates from Selected Causes with the Business Cycle, 1919-47," (Unpublished Ph.D. dissertation, Department of Sociology, University of Chicago, 1952).

8. See Appendix II, Table 4, for the trend line fitted to this index of deaths due to alcoholism.

9. The use of cause of death data appears to be a legitimate device for our purpose, in view of the marked tendency for victims of murder to be murdered by members of their own race. Sutherland notes that "in crimes of personal violence the victims and the offenders are generally of the same social group, and have residences not far apart. Negroes murder Negroes, Italians murder Italians, and Chinese murder Chinese." See Edwin H. Sutherland, *Principles of Criminology* (Chicago: J. B. Lippincott Co., 1947), p. 25. Harlan found that, of 500 consecutive homicides committed in Birmingham during the period from January, 1937, to December, 1944, "only 2.8 per cent . . . crossed race lines." See Howard Harlan, "Five Hundred Homicides," *Journal of Criminal Law and Criminology*, XL (March-April, 1950), p. 745. Garfinkel studied 673 instances of homicide which occurred in ten North Carolina counties during the period from 1930 to 1940. He found that 90.9 per cent of these homicides were intra-racial. See Harold Garfinkel, "Research Note on Inter- and Intra-Racial Homicides," *Social Forces*, XXVII (May, 1949), pp. 369-81. Von Hentig cites the study of Bruce and Fitzgerald in support of this view. See Hans Von Hentig, *The Criminal and His Victim* (New Haven: Yale University Press, 1948), pp. 394-5. These authors found that in Memphis, during the period 1920-25, out of all the white persons who were victims of murder, 73 per cent were killed by whites, 11 per cent were killed by non-whites, and the rest were killed by unknown assailants. Von Hentig refers to Andrew A. Bruce and Thomas S. Fitzgerald, *A Study of Crime in the City of Memphis, Tennessee* (Chicago, 1928). More recently, Vold has noted the "relatively close approximation" of

murder rates as reported to the Federal Bureau of Investigation, and homicide as a cause of death in the United States during the last decade as both of these reporting systems have more nearly approximated full coverage of the country. See George B. Vold, "Extent and Trend of Capital Crimes in the United States," *The Annals of the American Academy of Political and Social Science,* CCLXXXIV (November, 1952), pp. 1-7.

10. Using the conventional formula.

11. Arthur F. Raper, *The Tragedy of Lynching* (Chapel Hill: The University of North Carolina Press), p. 30. Raper found a correlation of —0.532 between the number of lynchings and the value of cotton in nine cotton states for the period, 1901-30.

12. See, for example, Durward Pruden, "A Sociological Study of a Texas Lynching," *Studies in Sociology,* Vol. I, No. 1 (1936), pp. 3-9, as reprinted in Logan Wilson and W. L. Kolb, *Sociological Analysis* (New York: Harcourt, Brace and Company, 1949), pp. 335-343.

13. U. S. Bureau of the Census, *Prisoners in State and Federal Prisons and Reformatories* (Washington: Government Printing Office, 1926 through 1941).

14. These correlations were obtained when trend was eliminated from Ayres' index by fitting a straight line to the data. When the trend of business was eliminated by fitting a second degree parabola to these data, the correlation for males became 0.01 and the correlation for females, 0.25.

▶ CHAPTER IV

1. We are using the term "ascriptive category" to refer to the major differentiations by sex, age, and income. Applicability of the term to sex and race poses no problem and the status position of the aged cannot be described as "achieved." Groups with high income include persons who have "achieved" their present economic position but the correlation between income position of fathers and sons permits use of the "ascriptive" status term for present purposes.

2. Karl Menninger, *Man Against Himself* (New York: Harcourt, Brace and Company, 1938).

3. Otto Fenichel, *The Psychoanalytic Theory of Neurosis* (New York: W. W. Norton, 1945), p. 400.

4. John Dollard, Leonard W. Doob, Neal E. Miller, O. H. Mowrer, and Robert F. Sears, *Frustration and Aggression* (New Haven: Yale University Press, 1939), p. 47.

5. *Ibid.,* p. 1. This statement has been questioned by a number of writers. Faris, for example, lists over a dozen possible consequences to frustration. He states: "A book could be written about aggression as the answer to frustration, and several such books have been written.

This outcome is of the highest importance and has its collective as well as individual manifestations. But unless what I have written here is wholly erroneous, aggression is not the only outcome of frustration." See Ellsworth Faris, "Some Results of Frustration," *Sociology and Social Research*, XXXI (November-December, 1946), p. 90. It may be noted that our argument does not rest on the assumption that aggression is the only consequence of frustration. There is no absence of consensus about the fact that aggression is one highly important consequence of frustration.

6. Dollard, Doob, Miller, Mowrer, and Sears, *op. cit.*, p. 11.

7. *Ibid.*, p. 6.

8. Samuel A. Stouffer, *et al.*, *The American Soldier* (Princeton: Princeton University Press, 1949), I and II; and Robert K. Merton and Alice S. Kitt, "Contributions to the Theory of Reference Group Behavior," *Continuities in Social Research*, ed. by Robert K. Merton and Paul F. Lazarsfeld (Glencoe, Illinois: The Free Press, 1950).

9. Samuel A. Stouffer and Paul F. Lazarsfeld, *Research Memorandum on the Family in the Depression* (New York: Social Science Research Council, Bulletin No. 29, 1937), pp. 28-35.

10. Economists have shown that the ratio of the number of "additional workers," (persons who are on the labor market because of the unemployment of the usual breadwinner in the family and who otherwise would not be seeking work) to the number of unemployed usual workers rises during business depression. See, for example, W. S. Woytinsky, *Additional Workers and the Volume of Unemployment in the Depression* (Washington: Committee on Social Security, Social Science Research Council, 1940).

11. St. Clair Drake and Horace R. Cayton, *Black Metropolis* (New York: Harcourt, Brace and Company, 1945), p. 557, *et passim*.

12. Horst Mendershausen, *Changes in Income Distribution During the Great Depression* (New York: National Bureau of Economic Research, 1946).

13. Coefficients of variation increase, however, reflecting the smaller proportionate declines in the standard deviation as compared with the mean.

14. Mendershausen, *op. cit.*, p. 119.

▶ CHAPTER V

1. Emile Durkheim, *Suicide,* trans. John A. Spaulding and George Simpson (Glencoe, Illinois: The Free Press, 1951), p. 257.

2. Data are for white persons only, eliminating the danger that the result is a function of the higher proportion of Negroes in the enlisted ranks.

3. Durkheim, *op. cit.*, p. 258.

4. *Ibid.,* p. 208.

5. Single females aged 75 and over have a rate of 5.5 per 100,000 while married females of this age group have a rate of 6.0 per 100,000. Data from National Office of Vital Statistics, Federal Security Agency, *Vital Statistics—Special Reports: Deaths from Selected Causes by Marital Status, by Age and Sex, United States, 1940* (Washington: Government Printing Office, October, 1947), p. 162.

6. Durkheim, *op. cit.,* p. 209.

7. Max Weber, *The Theory of Social and Economic Organization,* trans. A. M. Henderson and Talcott Parsons (New York: Oxford University Press, 1947), p. 168.

8. See Ruth S. Cavan, *Suicide* (Chicago: University of Chicago Press, 1928), pp. 77-105; aslo Calvin F. Schmid, "Suicides in Seattle, 1914-1925: An Ecological and Behavioristic Study," *University of Washington Publications in the Social Sciences,* V (October, 1928).

9. See Louis I. Dublin, Alfred J. Lotka, and Mortimer Spiegelman, *Length of Life* (New York: The Ronald Press Company, 1949), pp. 262-266, for the method of computing the per cent of paternal orphans. See also, A. J. Lotka, "Orphanhood in Relation to Demographic Factors: A Study in Populational Analysis," *Metron,* IX (1931-32).

▶ CHAPTER VI

1. See footnote 9, Chapter III, for a justification of the use of mortality statistics to index the relative incidence of homicide committed by Negroes and whites.

2. Edwin H. Sutherland, *Principles of Criminology* (Chicago: J. B. Lippincott Company, 1947), p. 120.

3. For a recent documentation of regional variations of capital crimes in the United States, see George B. Vold, "Extent and Trend of Capital Crimes in the United States," *The Annals of the American Academy of Political and Social Science,* Vol. 284 (November, 1952), pp. 1-7.

4. Adapted from U. S. Federal Bureau of Investigation, *Uniform Crime Reports for the United States and its Possessions,* Vol. XXII, No. 2 (1951) (Washington: Government Printing Office, 1952), Table 31.

5. Cf., Harry Elmer Barnes and Negley K. Teeters, *New Horizons in Criminology* (New York: Prentice-Hall, Inc., 1951), p. 128; and Walter C. Reckless, *The Crime Problem* (New York: Appleton-Century Crofts, Inc., 1950), p. 95.

6. Sutherland, *op. cit.,* pp. 134-135.

7. Austin L. Porterfield, "Suicide and Crime in the Social Structure of an Urban Setting: Fort Worth, 1930-1950," *American Sociological Review,* XVII (June, 1952), p. 341. Alpert has used life insurance statistics of suicide and homicide rates among Ordinary and Industrial

policy holders to indicate the same relationship. See Harry Alpert, "Suicides and Homicides," *American Sociological Review,* XV (October, 1950), p. 673.

8. *Uniform Crime Reports, op. cit., passim.*

9. Porterfield, *op. cit.,* p. 344 f. Recent research by Miller and Swanson bears upon Porterfield's findings. In their studies of adolescent boys in the Detroit public schools they find that the "general defensive distortions" of lower income and occupation level children are "extrapunitive," while these distortions of middle level children are "intrapunitive." See Daniel R. Miller and Guy E. Swanson, "Studies Relating Mechanisms of Defense to Levels of Income and Occupation," paper read at the annual meeting of the American Sociological Society, Berkeley, California, August 31, 1953.

10. See *Uniform Crime Reports, op. cit.,* Vol. XXI, No. 2, p. 107.

11. U. S. Bureau of the Census, *Prisoners in State and Federal Prisons and Reformatories* (Washington: Government Printing Office, 1940).

12. The proportion of men and women who are committed to prison for any given offense may of course be a function of fluctuations in other offenses. The consistency of the ratios obtained suggests that this is not true in the case under consideration. Failure to detect women in other offenses, e.g., shoplifting, may also lead to a spuriously high proportion of women offenders being imprisoned for homicide. But this may also be true of men. Regarding the incidence of homicide among women, Pollak presents evidence from the United States and from other countries pointing up the fact that "the woman who kills uses poison more often than other means" and that "they also use it more frequently than men." See Otto Pollak, *The Criminality of Women* (Philadelphia: University of Pennsylvania Press, 1950), pp. 16-19, *et passim.* Pollak stresses the fact that the use of poison as a means for perpetrating homicide, taken together with the social roles played by women in society, provides additional evidence of the greater concealment of female homicide. That is, such roles as housewife and mother, nurse, servant, and secretary, lend themselves to secrecy in the performance of many crimes, perhaps especially to homicide by way of poison.

13. Emil Frankel, "One Thousand Murders," *Journal of Criminal Law and Criminology,* XXIX (January-February, 1939), p. 684.

14. These data are not as reliable as we would wish, since the population base is the entire United States and the homicide and aggravated assault data are for only those jurisdictions reporting to the Federal Bureau of Investigation. The error introduced, however, may be assumed to be distributed randomly over the eight age groups.

. 15. The difference by sex in the direction of expression of aggression may also be related to psychological factors arising from dependency of children of both sexes primarily upon the mother in the early years of life. In particular, see Talcott Parsons, "The Social Structure of the Family," *The Family: Its Function and Destiny.* Ruth N. Anshen (New York: Harper and Brothers, 1949), pp. 186-88.

16. *Uniform Crime Reports, op. cit., passim.*

17. George B. Vold, "Crime in City and Country Areas," *The Annals of the American Academy of Political and Social Science,* CCXVII (September, 1941), pp. 38-45.

18. *Ibid.,* p. 41. The average rate was 1.4 per 100,000 population for the three year period, 1936-38.

19. P. A. Sorokin, C. C. Zimmerman, and C. J. Galpin, *A Systematic Source Book in Rural Sociology* (Minneapolis, University of Minnesota Press, 1930), II, pp. 266-86.

20. The negative relation tentatively established between homicide and urbanism is the first instance.

21. Calvin F. Schmid, "A Study of Homicides in Seattle, 1914 to 1924," *Social Forces,* IV (June, 1946), p. 749.

22. Howard Harlan, "Five Hundred Homicides," *The Journal of Criminal Law and Criminology,* XL (March-April, 1950), pp. 737-52.

23. Stuart Lottier, "Distribution of Criminal Offenses in Metropolitan Regions," *Journal of Criminal Law and Criminology,* XXIX (May-June, 1938), pp. 37-50.

24. A number of descriptions of underworld culture have been published. With particular reference to attitudes toward violence, see Barnes and Teeters, *op. cit.,* pp. 30 ff; also Danny Ahern, *How to Commit a Murder* (New York: Washburn Press, 1930); and B. B. Turkus and Sid Feder, *Murder, Inc.* (New York: Farrar, Straus, and Young, 1951).

25. Emile Durkheim, *Suicide,* trans. John A. Spaulding and George Simpson (Glencoe, Illinois: The Free Press, 1951), p. 354.

► CHAPTER VII

1. Sigmund Freud, *The Ego and the Id,* trans. John Riviere (London: The Hogarth Press, 1947), pp. 44-45.

2. Albert J. Reiss, "Social Correlates of Psychological Types of Delinquency," *American Sociological Review,* XVII (December, 1952), pp. 710-18.

3. Albert J. Reiss, "Delinquency as the Failure of Personal and Social Controls," *American Sociological Review,* XVI (April, 1951), pp. 196-207.

4. August Aichhorn, *Wayward Youth* (New York: The Viking Press, 1935), pp. 223-24.

5. Anna Freud, *The Ego and the Mechanisms of Defense,* trans. Cecil Baines (New York: International Universities Press, Inc., 1946), pp. 124-25.

6. *Ibid.,* p. 129.

7. Donald W. MacKinnon, "Violation of Prohibitions," *Explorations in Personality*. H. A. Murray *et al*. (New York: Oxford University Press, 1938), pp. 491-501.

8. C. M. Heinicke, "Some Antecedents and Correlates of Guilt and Fear in Young Boys," (Unpublished Ph.D. dissertation, Department of Social Relations, Harvard University, 1953), pp. 77-79.

9. Stanley H. King, "Emotional and Cardiovascular Responses During Stress—An Experimental Study," (Unpublished Ph.D. dissertation, Department of Social Relations, Harvard University, 1953).

10. Aichhorn, *op. cit.*, p. 202.

11. Heinicke, *op. cit.*, pp. 56-57.

12. Sigmund Freud, "The Passing of the Oedipus-Complex," *Collected Papers*, II, ed. E. Jones (London: The Hogarth Press, 1950), p. 273.

13. Sigmund Freud, *The Ego and the Id*, p. 45.

14. Otto Fenichel, *The Psychoanalytic Theory of Neurosis* (New York: W. W. Norton, 1945), p. 102.

15. J. W. M. Whiting and I. L. Child, *Child Training and Personality* (New Haven: Yale Universities Press, 1953).

16. Heinicke, *op. cit.*, p. 61-64.

17. Heinicke, *op. cit.*, pp. 64-67.

18. Stanley H. King and Andrew F. Henry, "The Expression of Aggression and Cardiovascular Reactions as Related to Parental Control over Behavior," (Unpublished Manuscript, 1954).

19. Talcott Parsons, "The Superego and the Theory of Social Systems," *Working Papers in the Theory of Action*. Talcott Parsons, Robert F. Bales and Edward A. Shils (Glencoe, Illinois: The Free Press, 1953), p. 17.

20. Fenichel, *op. cit.*, p. 102.

21. *Deaths from Selected Causes by Marital Status, by Age and Sex. United States, 1940*, U. S. Bureau of the Census (Washington: Government Printing Office, 1945).

22. *Criminal Statistics, England and Wales, 1949*, (London: His Majesty's Stationery Office, 1950), p. xx.

23. Ralph M. Patterson, "Psychiatric Study of Juveniles Involved in Homicide," *American Journal of Orthopsychiatry*, XIII (January, 1943), p. 129.

24. Ralph S. Banay, "Study of A Murder for Revenge," *Journal of Criminal Psychopathology*, III (July, 1941), pp. 1-10.

25. Alvin F. Meyers, Carl Sugar, and Benjamin Apfelberg, "Men Who Kill Women," *Journal of Clinical Psychopathology*, VII (January, 1946), p. 513.

26. W. I. Thomas and Dorothy Swaine Thomas, *The Child in America* (New York: Alfred A. Knopf, 1928), p. 572.

27. Part of the suicide-homicide variation by class possibly may turn

out to be a spurious function of the still largely unexplored relation between social class and child-rearing practices. *Within* each category, the person committing suicide or homicide may very well represent a particular psychological type yet the gross differences *between* many categories (such as those between the young and the old) certainly cannot be explained in this way.

▶ CHAPTER VIII

1. Stanley H. King, "Emotional and Cardiovascular Responses During Stress—An Experimental Study," (Unpublished Ph.D. dissertation, Department of Social Relations, Harvard University, 1953).
2. John W. Thibaut and Henry W. Riecken, "Authoritarianism, Status and the Communication of Aggression," *Human Relations* (In Press).

▶ APPENDIX I

1. Emile Durkheim, *Suicide,* trans. John A. Spaulding and George Simpson (Glencoe, Illinois: The Free Press, 1951), pp. 252-254.
2. *Ibid.,* p. 257.
3. *Ibid.,* p. 254.
4. Ibid., p. 258.
5. Maurice Halbwachs, *Les Causes du Suicide* (Paris: Libraire Felix Alcan, 1930).
6. Karl Menninger, *Man Against Himself* (New York: Harcourt, Brace and Company, 1938), p. 24.
7. *Ibid.,* p. 32.
8. Otto Fenichel, *The Psychoanalytic Theory of Neurosis* (New York: W. W. Norton, 1945), p. 400.
9. William F. Ogburn and Dorothy S. Thomas, "The Influence of the Business Cycle on Certain Social Conditions," *Journal of the American Statistical Association* XVIII (September, 1922), pp. 305-340.
10. Dorothy S. Thomas, *Social Aspects of the Business Cycle* (New York: Alfred A. Knopf, 1927), p. 73.
11. *Ibid.,* p. 114.
12. Louis I. Dublin and Bessie Bunzel, *To Be or Not To Be* (New York: Harrison Smith and Robert Haas, 1933), pp. 102-104.
13. *Ibid.,* pp. 105-106.
14. Ruth S. Cavan, *Suicide* (Chicago: University of Chicago Press, 1928), pp. 77-105.
15. Calvin F. Schmid, "Suicides in Seattle, 1914-1925: An Ecological and Behavioristic Study," *University of Washington Publications in the Social Sciences,* V (October, 1928).

16. U. S. Bureau of the Census, *Sixteenth Census of the United States: 1940, Vital Statistics Rates in the United States, 1900-1940* (Washington: Government Printing Office, 1943), p. 537.

17. *Ibid.,* p. 537.

18. Dublin and Bunzel, *op. cit.,* p. 406.

19. *Vital Statistics Rates in the United States, 1900-1940, op. cit.,* p. 537 ff.

20. Data from *Vital Statistics—Special Reports:* "Deaths from Selected Causes by Marital Status, By Age and Sex, United States, 1940." National Office of Vital Statistics, Federal Security Agency, Washington, D. C. (October, 1947), p. 162.

21. Dublin and Bunzel, *op. cit.,* pp. 96-97.

22. *Ibid.,* pp. 97-100.

23. Andrew F. Henry, "The Nature of the Relation Between Suicide and the Business Cycle," (Unpublished Ph.D. dissertation, Department of Sociology, University of Chicago, 1950).

24. Durkheim, *op. cit.* Bk. III, chap. ii.

25. Austin L. Porterfield, "Suicide and Crime in the Social Structure of an Urban Setting: Fort Worth, 1930-1950," *American Sociological Review,* XVII (June, 1952), pp. 344-345. See also Austin L. Porterfield and Robert W. Talbert, *Crime, Suicide and Social Well-Being in Your State and City* (Fort Worth: Leo Potishman Foundation, 1948).

26. William F. Ogburn, "The Great Man Versus Social Forces," *Social Forces,* V (December, 1926).

27. William A. Bonger, *Criminality and Economic Conditions,* trans. Henry P. Horton (Boston: Little, Brown and Company, 1916).

28. Hector Denis, *La Depression Economique et Sociale et L'histoire des Prix* (Brussels: G. J. Huysmans, 1895).

29. Thomas, *op. cit.,* p. 37.

30. Ogburn and Thomas, *op. cit.*

31. George R. Davies, "Social Aspects of the Business Cycle," *Quarterly Journal of the University of North Dakota,* XII (January, 1922), pp. 107-121.

32. Thomas, *op. cit.,* p. 161. Short has studied the relations between crimes and business conditions in England and Wales between 1920 and 1938, using indices of crimes known to the police as well as prosecutions. The findings are corroborative of Thomas' earlier work, though somewhat larger positive correlations between crimes of violence against the person and business are reported than those found by Thomas. See James F. Short, Jr., "A Social Aspect of the Business Cycle Re-examined: Crimes," *Research Studies of the State College of Washington,* XX (June, 1952), published as Proceedings of the Pacific Sociological Society, 1952, pp. 36-41.

33. L. Radzinowicz, "The Influence of Economic Conditions on Crime," *Sociological Review,* XXXIII (July and October, 1941).

34. *Ibid.,* p. 151.

35. See, for example, Harold A. Phelps, "Cycles of Crime," *Journal of the American Institute of Criminal Law and Criminology,* XX (May-June 1929), pp. 107-121; Mary Van Kleek, "Note on Fluctuations in Employment and in Crime in New York State," *Report on the Causes of Crime,* I National Commission on Law Observance and Enforcement (Washington: Government Printing Office, 1931); Albert C. Wagner, "Crime and Economic Change in Philadelphia, 1925-1934," *Journal of Criminal Law and Criminology,* XXVII (November-December, 1936), pp. 483-490; and Ray Mars Simpson, "The Employment Index, Arrests, Court Actions, and Commitments in Illinois," *Journal of Criminal Law and Criminology,* XXIV (January-February, 1934), pp. 914-922; and Ray Mars Simpson, "Unemployment and Prison Commitments," *Journal of Criminal Law and Criminology,* XXIV (September-October, 1932), pp. 404-14.

► APPENDIX II

1. For a description of this technique, see Appendix III.

2. Hubert R. Kemp, "Mathematical Treatment by Dorothy Swaine Thomas of Social Data Arranged in Time Series," *Methods in Social Science—A Case Book,* ed. by Stuart A. Rice (Chicago: University of Chicago Press, 1931), p. 573.

3. Wesley C. Mitchell, *Business Cycles: The Problem and Its Setting,* National Bureau of Economic Research, Inc. (New York: H. Wolff, 1927), p. 468.

4. "American Business Activity Since 1790" (23rd ed.; Cleveland, Ohio: The Cleveland Trust Company, 1950), p. 1. We have used this index as expressed in terms of the 1923/24/25 average equal to 100. These basic data, unfitted for trend, were sent to the writers by the Cleveland Trust Company.

5. Arthur F. Burns and Wesley C. Mitchell, *Measuring Business Cycles,* National Bureau of Economic Research, Inc. (New York: H. Wolff, 1946), pp. 98-99, *et passim.*

6. Numerous attempts have been made to discover cyclical change among social phenomena, but most of these have referred to cycles on a grand scale, as exemplified by Pitirim A. Sorokin, *Social and Cultural Dynamics* (New York: American Book Company, 1937-41) I-IV. On a smaller scale are such works as: Jane Richardson and A. L. Kroeber, "Three Centuries of Women's Dress Fashions: A Quantitative Analysis," *Anthropological Records,* V (1940); Robert K. Merton, "Fluctuations in the Rate of Industrial Invention," *Quarterly Journal of Economics* (May, 1935); and the various studies of the business cycle and its social impact which are discussed in this volume.

7. *The College Standard Dictionary of the English Language* (New York: Funk & Wagnalls Company, 1941), p. 1194.

8. Burns and Mitchell, *op. cit.*, p. 78.

► APPENDIX III

1. Arthur F. Burns and Wesley C. Mitchell, *Measuring Business Cycles,* National Bureau of Economic Research, Inc. (New York: H. Wolff, 1946).

2. *Ibid.*, pp. 11-12.

3. *Ibid.*, pp. 78-79.

4. *Ibid.* See chap. ii for a readable summary of the statistical analysis.

5. Sampling variability of the finding that 8 out of 11 cycles are "corresponding" is large. Ninety-five per cent confidence limits of the 8/11 proportion are .39 and .94.

6. The "mean" of a cycle is the total number of suicides during a cycle, divided by the length of the cycle in years.

► APPENDIX IV

1. The technique developed by Burns and Mitchell is explained in detail in Appendix III.

► APPENDIX V

1. The consideration of crimes against property has been limited to offenses of violence involving burglary and robbery.

2. The ten cities include Baltimore, Chicago, Cleveland, Cincinnati, Denver, Detroit, Kansas City (Kansas), Los Angeles, Rochester (N. Y.), and Wichita.

3. As explained in Appendix II, large cycles of business for the periods, 1929-41/1946-49, and 1930-41/1946/49, are isolated by fitting straight line trends to Ayres' index for these periods. Second degree parabolae, fitted to these same series, isolate small cycles of business. Small cycles are also isolated when a straight line trend is fitted to Ayres' index for the periods, 1929-41, and 1930-41. See Appendix II, Table 3, for the equations of these trends.

4. It has been suggested elsewhere that the unprecedented volume of public relief administered between the years, 1934-40, had the effect of "depressing" crimes against property which would otherwise have been at a high level during this business depression period. Burglaries rose sharply between 1929 and 1932, but dropped off rapidly after 1933,

more so than would be expected from the recovery of business during this period. See James F. Short, Jr., "A Note on Relief Programs and Crimes During the Depression of the 1930's," *American Sociological Review,* XVII (April, 1952), pp. 226-29.

5. These cities are substantially the same as the fifty-five cities comprising the second murder index listed in Chapter III (see Table 1, footnote b), with these exceptions: burglary data are not available for Newark (N. J.), and San Francisco, while burglary data are available for Lowell (Mass.), and Richmond (Va.).

6. Reference is made to the index of robberies known to the police in 11 cities. These cities are: Baltimore, Boston, Chicago, Cincinnati, Cleveland, Denver, Detroit, Kansas City (Kansas), Los Angeles, Rochester (N. Y.), and Wichita. This is the only robbery index examined in the present study. An analysis of robbery in fifty-six cities, similar to the fifty-five city burglary index, revealed discrepancies in pattern followed which led to its rejection for this study. See James F. Short, Jr., "An Investigation of the Relation Between Crime and Business Cycles," *op. cit.,* pp. 73 ff.

7. L. Radzinowicz, "The Influence of Economic Conditions on Crime," *Sociological Review,* XXXIII (July and October, 1941), p. 150.

8. See the discussion in Chapter IV.

Ahearn, Danny. *How to Commit a Murder*. New York: Washburn Press, 1930.

Aichhorn, August. *Wayward Youth*. New York: The Viking Press, 1935.

Alpert, Harry. "Suicides and Homicides," *American Sociological Review*, XV (October, 1950), p. 673.

"American Business Activity Since 1790." 23rd ed. Cleveland, Ohio: The Cleveland Trust Company, 1950.

Angell, Robert Cooley. *The Family Encounters the Depression*. New York: Charles Scribner's Sons, 1936.

Banay, Ralph S. "Study of A Murder for Revenge," *Journal of Criminal Psychopathology*, III (July, 1941), pp. 1-10.

Barnes, Harry Elmer, and Teeters, Negley K. *New Horizons in Criminology: The American Crime Problem*. New York: Prentice-Hall, Inc., 1951.

Bonger, William A. *Criminality and Economic Conditions*. Translated by Henry P. Horton. Boston: Little, Brown and Co., 1916.

Burns, Arthur F., and Mitchell, Wesley C. *Measuring Business Cycles*. National Bureau of Economic Research, Inc., New York: H. Wolff, 1946.

Cavan, Ruth S. *Suicide*. Chicago: University of Chicago Press, 1928.

Cavan, Ruth S., and Ranck, Katherine Howland. *The Family and the Depression*. Chicago: University of Chicago Press, 1938.

Cavan, Ruth S., *et al. Personal Adjustment in Old Age*. Chicago: Science Research Associates, 1949.

Criminal Statistics, England and Wales, 1949. London: His Majesty's Stationery Office, 1950.

Davies, George R. "Social Aspects of the Business Cycle," *Quarterly Journal of the University of North Dakota*, XII (January, 1922), pp. 107-21.

Denis, Hector. *La Depression Economique et Sociale et L'histoire des Prix*. Brussels: G. J. Huysmans, 1895.

Dollard, John, Doob, Leonard W., Miller, Neal E., Mowrer, O. H., and Sears, Robert F. *Frustration and Aggression.* New Haven: Yale University Press, 1939.

Drake, St. Clair, and Cayton, Horace R. *Black Metropolis.* New York: Harcourt, Brace & Co., 1945.

Dublin, Louis I., and Bunzel, Bessie. *To Be or Not To Be.* New York: Harrison Smith and Robert Haas, 1933.

Dublin, Louis I., Lotka, Alfred J., and Spiegelman, Mortimer. *Length of Life.* New York: The Ronald Press Co., 1949.

Durkheim, Emile. *Suicide.* Translated by John A. Spaulding and George Simpson. Glencoe, Illinois: The Free Press, 1951.

Faris, Ellsworth. "Some Results of Frustration," *Sociology and Social Research,* XXXI (November-December, 1946), pp. 87-92.

Fenichel, Otto. *The Psychoanalytic Theory of Neurosis.* New York: W. W. Norton, 1945.

Frankel, Emil. "One Thousand Murders," *Journal of Criminal Law and Criminology,* XXIX (January-February, 1939), pp. 672-88.

Frazier, E. Franklin. *The Negro Family in the United States.* Chicago: University of Chicago Press, 1939.

Freud, Anna. *The Ego and the Mechanisms of Defense.* Translated by Cecil Baines. New York: International Universities Press, Inc., 1946.

Freud, Sigmund. "The Passing of the Oedipus-Complex," *Collected Papers,* Vol. II. Edited by E. Jones. London: Hogarth Press, 1950.

Freud, Sigmund. *The Ego and the Id.* Translated by Joan Riviere. London: The Hogarth Press, 1947.

Funkenstein, D. H., and Greenblatt, M. "Nor-epinephrine-like and Epine-phrine-like Substances and the Elevation of Blood Pressure during Acute Stress," *Journal of Nervous and Mental Diseases,* (In Press).

Funkenstein, D. H., King, S. H., and Drolette, M. "The Experimental Evocation of Stress," *Symposium on Stress.* National Research Council and the Army Medical Graduate School, (In Press).

Garfinkel, Harold. "Research Note on Inter- and Intra-Racial Homicides," *Social Forces,* XXVII (May, 1949), pp. 369-81.

Halbwachs, Maurice. *Les Causes du Suicide.* Paris: Libraire Felix Alcan, 1930.

Harlan, Howard. "Five Hundred Homicides," *Journal of Criminal Law and Criminology,* XL (March-April, 1950), pp. 736-52.

Heinicke, C. "Some Antecedents and Correlates of Guilt and Fear in Young Boys." Unpublished Ph.D. dissertation, Department of Social Relations, Harvard University, 1953.

Henry, Andrew F. "The Nature of the Relation Between Suicide and the Business Cycle." Unpublished Ph.D. dissertation, Department of Sociology, University of Chicago, 1950.

Kemp, Hubert R. "Mathematical Treatment by Dorothy Swaine Thomas of Social Data Arranged in Time Series," *Methods in Social Science —A Case Book.* Edited by Stuart A. Rice. Chicago: University of Chicago Press, 1931.

King, Stanley H. "Emotional and Cardiovascular Responses during Stress —An Experimental Study." Unpublished Ph.D. dissertation, Department of Social Relations, Harvard University, 1953.

King, Stanley H., and Henry, Andrew F. "The Expression of Aggression and Cardiovascular Reactions as Related to Parental Control over Behavior." Unpublished manuscript, 1954.

Komarovsky, Mirra. *The Unemployed Man and His Family.* New York: The Dryden Press, Inc., 1940.

Linn, Erwin L. "The Correlation of Death Rates from Selected Causes with the Business Cycle, 1919-1947." Unpublished Ph.D. dissertation, Department of Sociology, University of Chicago, 1952.

Lotka, Alfred J. "Orphanhood in Relation to Demographic Factors: A Study in Population Analysis," *Metron,* IX (August, 1931), pp. 37-109.

Lottier, Stuart. "Distribution of Criminal Offenses in Metropolitan Regions," *Journal of Criminal Law and Criminology,* XXIX (May-June, 1938), pp. 37-50.

MacKinnon, Donald W. "Violation of Prohibitions," *Explorations in Personality.* Murray, H. A. *et al.* New York: Oxford University Press, 1938.

Mendershausen, Horst. *Changes in Income Distribution during the Great Depression.* New York: National Bureau of Economic Research, 1946.

Menninger, Karl. *Man Against Himself.* New York: Harcourt, Brace & Co., 1938.

Merton, Robert K. "Fluctuations in the Rate of Industrial Invention," *Quarterly Journal of Economics,* XLIX (May, 1935), pp. 454-69.

Merton, Robert K., and Kitt, Alice S. "Contributions to the Theory of Reference Group Behavior," *Continuities in Social Research.* Edited by Robert K. Merton and Paul F. Lazarsfeld. Glencoe, Illinois: The Free Press, 1950.

Meyers, Alvin F., Sugar, Carl, and Apfelberg, Benjamin. "Men Who Kill Women," *Journal of Clinical Psychopathology,* VII (January, 1946), pp. 443-72.

Miller, Daniel R., and Swanson, Guy E. "Studies Relating Mechanisms of Defense to Levels of Income and Occupation," paper read at the annual meeting of the American Sociological Society, Berkeley, California, August 31, 1953.

Mitchell, Wesley, C. *Business Cycles: The Problem and Its Setting.* New York: National Bureau of Economic Research, Inc., 1927.

Myrdal, Gunnar. *An American Dilemma.* New York: Harper and Brothers, 1944.

Ogburn, William F. "The Great Man versus Social Forces," *Social Forces,* V (December, 1926), pp. 225-31.

Ogburn, William F., and Thomas, Dorothy S. "The Influence of the Business Cycle on Certain Social Conditions," *Journal of the American Statistical Association,* XVIII (September, 1922), pp. 305-50.

Parsons, Talcott. "Age and Sex in the Social Structure of the United States," *American Sociological Review,* VII (October, 1942), pp. 604-16.

Parsons, Talcott. "An Analytical Approach to the Theory of Social Stratification," *Essays in Sociological Theory, Pure and Applied.* Glencoe, Illinois: The Free Press, 1949.

Parsons, Talcott. "The Social Structure of the Family," *The Family: Its Function and Destiny.* Ruth N. Anshen. New York: Harper and Brothers, 1949.

Parsons, Talcott. "The Superego and the Theory of Social Systems," *Working Papers in the Theory of Action.* Talcott Parsons, Robert F. Bales and Edward A. Shils. Glencoe, Illinois: The Free Press, 1953.

Parsons, Talcott, and Shils, Edward A. *Toward a General Theory of Action.* Cambridge: Harvard University Press, 1951.

Patterson, Ralph M. "Psychiatric Study of Juveniles Involved in Homicide," *American Journal of Orthopsychiatry,* XIII (January, 1943), pp. 125-29.

Phelps, Harold A. "Cycles of Crime," *Journal of Criminal Law and Criminology,* XX (May-June, 1929), pp. 107-21.

Pollak, Otto. *The Criminality of Women.* Philadelphia: University of Pennsylvania Press, 1950.

Porterfield, Austin L. "Personality, Crime, and the Cultural Pattern," *Current Approaches to Delinquency.* New York: National Probation and Parole Association, 1949.

Porterfield, Austin L. "Suicide and Crime in the Social Structure of an Urban Setting: Fort Worth, 1930-1950," *American Sociological Review,* XVII (June, 1952), pp. 341-49.

Porterfield, Austin L., and Talbert, Robert W. *Crime, Suicide and Social Well-being in Your State and City.* Fort Worth: Leo Potishman Foundation, Texas Christian University, 1948.

Pruden, Durward, "A Sociological Study of a Texas Lynching," *Studies in Sociology,* I (1936), pp. 3-9.

Rado, S. "Emergency Behavior," *Anxiety.* Edited by P. H. Hoch and J. Zubin. Proceedings of the Thirty-ninth Annual Meeting of the American Psychopathological Association, 1949. New York: Grune and Stratton, 1950.

Radzinowicz, L. "The Influence of Economic Conditions on Crime—II," *The Sociological Review.* XXXIII (July-October, 1941), pp. 139-53.

Raper, Arthur F. *The Tragedy of Lynching.* Chapel Hill: The University of North Carolina Press, 1933.

Reckless, Walter C. *The Crime Problem.* New York: Appleton-Century Crofts, 1950.

Reiss, Albert J. "Social Correlates of Psychological Types of Delinquency," *American Sociological Review,* XVII (December, 1952), pp. 710-18.

Reiss, Albert J. "Delinquency as the Failure of Personal and Social Controls," *American Sociological Review,* XVI (April, 1951), pp. 196-207.

Richardson, Jane, and Kroeber, A. L. *Three Centuries of Women's Dress Fashions: A Quantitative Analysis.* Berkeley: University of California Press, 1940.

Robinson, W. S. "Ecological Correlations and the Behavior of Individuals," *American Sociological Review,* XV (June, 1950), pp. 351-57.

Schmid, Calvin F. " A Study of Homicides in Seattle, 1914-1924," *Social Forces,* IV (June, 1926), pp. 745-56.

Schmid, Calvin F. "Suicide in Seattle, 1914-1925; An Ecological and Behavioristic Study," *University of Washington Publications in the Social Sciences,* V (October, 1928).

Short, James F., Jr. "A Note on Relief Programs and Crimes during the Depression of the 1930's," *American Sociological Review,* XVII (April, 1952), pp. 226-29.

Short, James F., Jr. "An Investigation of tne Relation between Crime and Business Cycles," Unpublished Ph.D. dissertation, Department of Sociology, University of Chicago, 1951.

Short, James F., Jr. "A Social Aspect of the Business Cycle Re-examined: Crimes," *Research Studies of the State College of Washington.* Proceedings of the Pacific Sociological Society, 1952. XX (June, 1952), pp. 26-41.

Simpson, Ray Mars. "The Employment Index, Arrests, Court Actions, and Commitments in Illinois," *Journal of Criminal Law and Criminology,* XXIV (January-February, 1934), pp. 914-22.

Simpson, Ray Mars. "Unemployment and Prison Commitments," *Journal of Criminal Law and Criminology,* XXIII (September-October, 1932), pp. 404-14.

Sorokin, Pitirim A. *Social and Cultural Dynamics.* 4 vols. New York: American Book Co., 1937-1941.

Sorokin, Pitirim A., Zimmerman, Carle C., and Galpin, Charles J. *A Systematic Source Book in Rural Sociology.* Vol. II. Minneapolis: University of Minnesota Press, 1930.

Stouffer, Samuel A. *et al. The American Soldier.* 2 vols. Princeton: Princeton University Press, 1949.

Stouffer, Samuel A., and Lazarsfeld, Paul F. *Research Memorandum on the Family in the Depression.* New York: Social Science Research Council, Bulletin No. 29, 1937.

Sutherland, Edwin H. *Principles of Criminology.* 4th ed. Philadelphia: J. B. Lippincott Co., 1947.

Thibaut, John W., and Riecken, Henry W. "Authoritarianism, Status and the Communication of Aggression," *Human Relations* (In Press).

Thomas, Dorothy S. *Social Aspects of the Business Cycle.* New York: Alfred A. Knopf, 1927.

Thomas, W. I., and Thomas, Dorothy S., *The Child in America.* New York: Alfred A. Knopf, 1928.

Turkus, B. B., and Feder, Sid. *Murder, Inc.* New York: Farrar, Straus, and Young, 1951.

U. S. Bureau of the Census. *1950 Census of Population—Advanced Reports,* Series PC-14, No. 5. Washington: Government Printing Office, 1952.

U. S. Bureau of the Census. *Deaths from Selected Causes by Marital Status, By Age and Sex. United States, 1940.* Washington: Government Printing Office, 1945.

U. S. Bureau of the Census. *Prisoners in State and Federal Prisons and Reformatories,* Washington: Government Printing Office, 1926-1941.

U. S. Bureau of the Census. *Vital Statistics Rates in the United States, 1900-1940.* Washington: Government Printing Office, 1943.

U. S. Federal Bureau of Investigation. *Uniform Crime Reports for the United States and its Possessions,* Vol. XXI. Washington: Government Printing Office, 1950.

VanKleek, Mary. "Note on Fluctuations in Employment and in Crime in New York State," *Report on the Causes of Crime,* Vol. I. National Commission on Law Observance and Enforcement. Washington: Government Printing Office, 1931.

Vold, George B. "Crime in City and Country Areas," *The Annals of the American Academy of Political and Social Sciences,* CCXVII (September, 1941), pp. 38-45.

Vold, George B. "Extent and Trend of Capital Crimes in the United States," *The Annals of the American Academy of Political and Social Sciences,* CCLXXXIV (November, 1952), pp. 1-7.

Von Hentig, Hans. *The Criminal and His Victim.* New Haven: Yale University Press, 1948.

Wagner, Albert C. "Crime and Economic Change in Philadelphia, 1925-1934," *Journal of Criminal Law and Criminology,* XXVII (November-December, 1936), pp. 483-90.

Weber, Max. *The Theory of Social and Economic Organization.* Translated by A. M. Henderson and Talcott Parsons. New York: Oxford University Press, 1947.

Wertham, Frederic. *The Show of Violence.* New York: Doubleday & Co., 1949.

Wertham, Frederic. *Dark Legend: A Study in Murder.* New York: Duell, Sloan and Pearce, 1941.

Whiting, J. W. M., and Child, I. L. *Child Training and Personality.* New Haven: Yale Universities Press, 1953.

Wirth, Louis, and Bernert, Eleanor. *Locial Community Fact Book of Chicago.* Chicago, University of Chicago Press, 1949.

Wirth, Louis, and Furez, Margaret (eds.). *Local Community Fact Book, 1938.* A Report Prepared for the Chicago Recreation Commission. Chicago: Chicago Recreation Commission, 1938.

Woytinsky, W. S. *Additional Workers and the Volume of Unemployment in the Depression.* Washington: Committee on Social Security, Social Science Research Council, 1940.

Age
  correlation of suicide and business cycle by, 30, 36-38, 41
  homicide rates by, 88-89
  and relational system, 17-18, 77-78, 91, 125
  and status, 16, 24-25, 36-38, 70
  suicide rates by, 16, 70-71, 75
Aggravated assault, 47-53
Aggression
  against parents, 110-111
  cardio-vascular reaction during stress, 18, 106, 109-110, 113, 120-122, 126
  cultural differences in expression of, by sex, 88, 190 n. 15
  and external restraint, 18, 102-103, 119
  as factor in divorce, 116
  and guilt, 105, 108, 110
  inhibition of, 108, 113-115
  other-oriented, 13, 15-19, 102
  psychoanalytic theory of, 55, 104

  "psychological" legitimization of, 18-19, 103-106
  punishment, 108
  self-oriented, 13, 15-18, 55, 102, 110, 113
  and super-ego, 104-105
  target of, 65, 102
  and war, 122
Ahearn, Danny, 191
Aichhorn, August, 104, 106, 109, 112, 115, 191-192
Alcoholism
  correlation with business cycle, 15, 45, 47-51, 64
  and homicide, 15, 45, 47-51
  and race, 49-50
Alpert, Harry, 189-190
Altruistic suicide, 104
Angell, Robert Cooley, 184
Anomic suicide, 40-41
Anshen, Ruth N., 191
Apfelberg, Benjamn, 192
Ascribed status, 187 n. 1
Ayres, Leonard P., 25, 28, 38-39,

142, 145-147, 149, 169, 173-174, 183, 185, 187, 195-196

Banay, Ralph S., 192
Barnes, Harry Elmer, 189, 191
Bernert, Eleanor, 185
Bonger, William A., 138, 194
Bunzel, Bessie, 30, 71, 134, 137, 184, 193-194
Burgess, E. W., 11
Burglary, 174-177, 179-181
Burns, Arthur F., 141, 155, 157-158, 161-165, 167-168, 183, 195-196
Burns-Mitchell technique
  as applied to suicide of single persons, 156-162
  illustrated, 155-162, 164-173
Business cycle
  correlation with
    aggravated assault, 46-53
    alcoholism, 15, 45, 47-51, 64
    burglary, 174-177, 179-181
    homicide, 15, 45-55, 59-63
    lynching, 51, 53, 59
    robbery, 177-181
    suicide, 15, 23, 25-45, 54-55, 58
  effect on distribution of income, 63-64
  effect on status relationships, 14-15, 19, 27-28, 57-58
  frustration as consequence of, 14-15, 19, 23-24, 55-65, 181
  large cycles, 144-145, 174-181
  as objective source of frustration, 19, 54-64, 123
  and relative deprivation, 56-59
  small cycles, 146-147, 174-181
  techniques of measurement, 141-162
  trends, 141-143

Cardio-vascular reaction during

stress, 18, 106, 109-110, 113, 120-122, 126
  epinephrine-like, 106, 109-110, 120-122
  and guilt, 113-126
  maternal dominance, 106, 109-110
  nor-epinephrine-like, 106, 109, 120-122
Cathexis, 74, 112
Cavan, Ruth S., 17, 76, 134-135, 183-184, 189, 193
Cayton, Horace R., 60, 188
Child, I. L., 108-109, 113
Child-rearing practices by social class, 192 n. 27
Crime
  rates in Southern cities, 84
  review of previous contributions of fact, 139-140
  review of theoretical literature, 138
  see also aggravated assault, burglary, crimes against property, homicide, organized crime and robbery
Crimes against property, 196 n. 4
Cross-culture reference, 14
Cycles of suicide
  amplitude of, 158
  secular movements, 158

Davies, George R., 139, 194
Delinquency, 104
Denis, Hector, 138, 194
Depression
  effect on family, 37-38
  effect on sex groups, 56-57, 184 n. 31
Divorce, 115-116; *see also marital status*
Dollard, John, 55, 187-188
Doob, Leonard W., 55, 187-188
Drake, St. Clair, 60, 188

Dublin, Louis I., 30, 71, 134, 137, 184, 189, 193-194

Durkheim, Emile, 14-17, 23, 26-27, 42, 54, 62, 64, 69, 72-74, 80, 95, 104, 131-133, 183-184, 189, 191, 193-194

Ecological distribution
of homicide, 92-93
of suicide, 76
of suicide in Chicago, 38-41
Egoistic suicide, 40, 72-74
Epinephrine, 106, 109-110, 120-122
External restraint
and aggression, 18, 102-103, 119
and experimentally-induced frustration, 121-122
and homicide, 78, 82, 97, 119
operationally defined, 120-121
and organized crime, 94, 124-125
as primary basis of legitimization of aggression, 102-103
and status, 17-18, 70-72, 75, 103
and strength of relational system, 16-18, 74-78, 80, 91-92, 96, 103, 124-125
and suicide, 17-19, 75, 78, 119
and treatment of depressive mental patients, 126
and underworld, 94
vertical restraint, 80, 96
see also aggression, status, and relational system
Extra-punitiveness, 190 n. 9

Faris, Ellsworth, 187-188
Feder, Sid, 191
Fenichel, Otto, 55, 107, 133, 187, 192, 193
Frankel, Emil, 88, 90, 190
Frazier, E. Franklin, 184
Freud, Anna, 105-106, 191

Freud, Sigmund, 107, 109, 191-192
Frustration
as consequence of business cycle, 14-15, 19, 23-24, 55-65, 181
business cycle as objective source of, 19, 54-64, 123
definition, 55-56
experimentally-induced and external restraint, 121-122
frustration-aggression hypothesis, 14-15, 55, 187 n. 5
of racial groupings during business contraction, 60
see also aggression
Furez, Margaret, 185

Galpin, Charles J., 191
Garfinkel, Harold, 186
Geographic region
homicide rates by, 83-86
status as related to, 82
suicide rates by, 86
Guilt, 105, 108, 113, 126
and degree of nurturance, 108
and maternal dominance, 108
projection of, 118, 127
and withdrawal of love, 108, 110

Halbwachs, Maurice, 193
Harlan, Howard, 92, 186, 191
Heinicke, C., 105-106, 108-111, 191
Henry, Andrew F., 109-110, 185, 192, 194
Homicide
as aggressive act, 55, 64-65, 101
and alcoholism, 15, 45, 47-51
correlation with business cycle, 15, 45-55, 59-63
by race, 15, 48-53, 59-62
by sex, 52
by status categories, 45, 55, 59-63

ecological distribution, 92-93
and external restraint, 78, 82, 97, 119
joint occurrence with suicide, 116-117, 126-127
lynching as form of, 51, 53, 55
and marital status, 124
and organized crime, 90, 93-94
and parental mortality, 125
and projection, 117-118
psychoanalytic theory of, 13
rates by
  age, 88-89
  cities low in socio-economic status, 84-85
  geographic region, 83-86
  marital status, 18, 91, 95, 97
  race, 83, 87-88
  sex, 87, 89, 190 n. 12
  sex and race, 87-88
  urban and rural areas, 90-91
by race and sex, suggested research, 124
and relational system, 17-18, 78, 91, 95-97
and social control, 82-97
and status, 59, 82-89, 94-95, 123-124
during war, 102
Horizontal restraint, 80, 96

Identification with aggressor, 104-105
Income
correlation of suicide and business cycle by, 38-42
effect of business cycle on distribution of, 63-64
status as function of, 24-25, 38, 70
suicide rates by, 70-71
Internalization
and projection, 118, 127
and withdrawal of love, 108-109

Intra-punitiveness, 109 n. 9

Kemp, Hubert R., 195
King, Stanley H., 106, 109-110, 122, 192-193
Kitt, Alice S., 188
Komarovsky, Mirra, 37, 184
Kroeber, A. L., 195

Lazarsfeld, Paul F., 56, 184, 188
Linn, Erwin L., 48, 186
Lotka, Alfred J., 189
Lottier, Stuart, 92, 191
Lynching
correlation with business cycle, 51, 53, 55, 59
as form of homicide, 51, 53
and status, 51

MacKinnon, Donald W., 105, 192
MacRae, Duncan, Jr., 11
Manic-depression, 126
Marital status
correlation of suicide and business cycle by, 37-38
and homicide, suggested research, 124
homicide rates by, 18, 91, 95, 97
and relational system, 16, 75
suicide rates by, 73, 115
see also divorce and widowhood
Maternal dominance, 106, 108, 109-110
Mendershausen, Horst, 63, 188
Menninger, Karl, 55, 133, 187, 193
Merton, Robert K., 188, 195
Meyers, Alvin F., 117, 192
Miller, Daniel R., 190
Miller, Neal E., 55, 187-188
Mills, Theodore M., 11
Mitchell, Wesley C., 141, 155, 157-158, 161-165, 167-168, 183, 195-196
Mobility, 33-34, 63

Mowrer, O. H., 55, 187-188
Myrdal, Gunnar, 184

National Bureau of Economic Research, 142-143, 146, 163
Negroes
  migration of, 35
  prestige position of female, 87-88
  status of, 24-25, 32-35, 184 n. 22
  see also, lynching, race
Neurosis, 122
Nor-epinephrine, 106, 109-110, 120-122
Nurturance, 108, 111-112, 114-116, 126
  aggression as threat to, 18, 114-116, 126

Oedipus complex, 107
Ogburn, William F., 11, 134, 139, 141, 193-194
Organized crime, 90, 93-94, 124-125
Other-oriented aggression, 13, 15-19, 102

Parental mortality, 77-78, 125
Parsons, Talcott, 11, 24, 36, 112, 183-184, 190, 192
Patterson, Ralph M., 117, 192
Phelps, Harold A., 195
Pollak, Otto, 190
Porterfield, Austin L., 84-85, 137-138, 189, 190, 194
Projection of guilt, 127, 188
Pruden, Durward, 187
Psychoanalytic theory
  of aggression, 55, 104
  of homicide, 13
  of suicide, 13, 55, 104
Psychological legitimization of aggression, 18-19, 103-106
Public relief and crimes against property, 196 n. 4

Punishment, 106-108, 110-111; *see also withdrawal of love*
Race
  and alcoholism, 49-50
  correlation of homicide and business cycle by, 15, 48-53, 59-61
  correlation of suicide and business cycle by, 29-30, 32-36, 41
  effect of business cycle on racial groups, 57-58
  homicide by race and sex, suggested research, 124
  homicide rates by, 83, 87-88
  and status, 24-25, 32-35, 41, 52, 82, 184 n. 22
  suicide rates by, 70-71
  see also lynching, Negroes
Radzinowicz, L., 48, 139-140, 181, 186, 194, 197
Ranck, Katherine Howland, 184
Raper, Arthur F., 51, 187
Reckless, Walter C., 189
Reference dates, 156
Reiss, Albert J., 11, 104, 191
Relational system
  and age, 17-18, 77-78, 91, 125
  definition, 74
  in disorganized sections of cities, 16, 76-77, 92, 124-125
  and external restraint, 16-18, 74-78, 80, 91-92, 96, 103, 124-125
  and homicide, 17-18, 78, 91, 95-97
  and horizontal restraint, 80, 96
  and marital status, 16, 75
  and parental mortality, 77-78
  and status, 17
  social relationship as defined by Weber, 74
  and suicide, 16-17, 72
  and urbanism, 16, 91-92

Relative deprivation, 56-59
Religion, 14
Richardson, Jane, 195
Riecken, Henry W., 193
Robbery
during business expansion and contraction, 180-181
correlation with business cycle, 177-181
Robinson, W. S., 185
R-tables, 156

Schmid, Calvin F., 76, 92, 135, 189, 191-192
Sears, Robert F., 55, 187-188
Self-oriented aggression, 13, 15-18, 55, 102, 110, 113
and guilt, 113
and maternal dominance, 110
as residual category, 102
Severity of discipline, 106-107, 109, 114
Sex
correlation of homicide and business cycle by, 52
cultural difference in expression of aggression by, 88, 190 n. 15
correlation of suicide and business cycle by, 23, 27-34, 36-38, 41-44
homicide by race and sex, suggested research, 124
homicide rates by, 87-89, 190 n. 12
status as function of, 24-25, 27, 32- 33, 35, 52-53, 70, 184 n. 22
status of Negroes by, 32-33, 35, 184 n. 22
suicide at peaks and troughs of business cycle by, 30, 33, 42-43, 165, 167
suicide during expansion and

contraction phases of business by, 31-33, 168-171
suicide rates by, 70-71
Shils, Edward A., 184
Short, James F. Jr., 186, 194, 197
Simpson, Ray Mars, 195
Social class and child-rearing practices, 192 n. 27
Social control
and homicide, 82-97
and suicide, 69-81
Socialization, 111
Sorokin, Pitirim A., 91, 191, 195
Specific cycles
amplitude of, 156-158
definition, 156
Spiegelman, Mortimer, 189
S-tables, 156
Status
as block to upward mobility, 63
correlation of homicide and business cycle by, 45, 55, 59-63
correlation of suicide and business cycle by, 34-36, 41, 43-45, 54-55, 58
effect of business cycle on status relationships, 14-15, 19, 27-28, 57-58
and external restraint, 17-18, 70-72, 75, 103
and extra-punitiveness, 190 n. 9
as function of
age, 16, 24-25, 36-38, 70
income, 24-25, 38, 70
race, 24-25, 32-35, 41, 52, 82, 184 n. 22
religion, 14
region, 82-86
sex, 24-25, 27, 32-33, 35, 52-53, 70, 184 n. 22
and homicide, 59, 82-89, 94-95, 123-124
and intra-punitiveness, 190 n. 9

and lynching, 51
and relational system, 17
and suicide, 16, 59, 69, 123-124
suicide rates by, 70
of U. S. Army officers and enlisted men, 70
Stool pigeon, 93
Stouffer, Samuel A., 56, 184, 188
Sugar, Carl, 192
Suicide
as aggressive act, 55, 64-65, 101
altruistic, 104
analysis by Burns-Mitchell technique, 155-162, 164-173
anomic, 40-41
correlation with business cycle
by, 15, 23, 25-45, 54-55, 58
age, 30, 36-38, 41
income, 38-42
marital status, 37-38
race, 32-36, 41
sex, 23, 27-33, 36-38, 41-44
sex and age, 30, 36-38
sex and race, 29-30, 32-34, 41
status categories, 34-36, 41,
43-45, 54-55, 58
urban and rural areas, 34
during contraction and expansion
phases of business, 25-27,
31-33, 42-43, 54, 167-173
ecological distribution, 76
in Chicago, 38-41
egoistic, 40, 72-74
and external restraint, 17-19, 75,
78, 119
joint occurrence with homicide,
116-117, 126-127
and parental mortality, 77-78,
125
at peaks of business, 30, 33, 42-
43, 62, 163-167
psychoanalytic theory of, 13, 55,
104

rates by
age, 16, 70-71, 75
cities high in socio-economic
status, 84
geographic regions, 86
at given point in time, 69
income, 70-71
marital status, 73, 115
race, 70-71
sex, 70-71
status categories, 70
urban and rural areas, 76
widowed and divorced, 115-
116
and relational system, 16-17, 72
and relative deprivation, 57-58
and religion, 14
review of previous contributions
of fact, 134-138
review of theoretical literature,
131-134
at troughs of business, 25, 30,
33, 42-43, 163-167
and social control, 69-81
and status, 16, 59, 69, 123-124
and super-ego, 104-105
and war, 102
Super-ego
and cheating, 105
definition, 103
and delinquency, 104
and expression of aggression,
104-105
formation of, 104
and guilt, 105
and severity of discipline, 106-
107, 109, 114
strength of, 18
and suicide, 104-105
and withdrawal of love, 108
Sutherland, Edwin H., 83, 84, 186,
189
Swanson, Guy E., 190

Talbert, Robert W., 194
Teeters, Negley K., 189, 191
Thematic Apperception Test, 126
Thibaut, John W., 193
Thomas, Dorothy S., 47, 55, 134, 138-139, 141, 186, 192-194
Thomas, W. I., 118, 192
Time series of social data, 143-147
Turkus, B. B., 191

Underworld, 94
Urbanism, 34, 76, 91-92
United States Army, 70

VanKleek, Mary, 195
Vertical restraint, 80, 96

Vold, George, B., 90, 91, 186, 189, 191
Von Hentig, Hans, 186

Wagner, Albert C., 195
War, 102, 122
Weber, Max, 17, 74, 183, 189
Whiting, J. W. M., 108-109, 113, 192
Widowhood, 115-116
Wirth, Louis, 185
Withdrawal of love, 108-111
Woytinsky, W. S., 188

Zimmerman, Carle C., 91, 191

THE LITERATURE OF
DEATH AND DYING

Abrahamsson, Hans. **The Origin of Death:** Studies in African Mythology. 1951

Alden, Timothy. **A Collection of American Epitaphs and Inscriptions with Occasional Notes.** Five vols. in two. 1814

Austin, Mary. **Experiences Facing Death.** 1931

Bacon, Francis. **The Historie of Life and Death with Observations Naturall and Experimentall for the Prolongation of Life.** 1638

Barth, Karl. **The Resurrection of the Dead.** 1933

Bataille, Georges. **Death and Sensuality:** A Study of Eroticism and the Taboo. 1962

Bichat, [Marie François] Xavier. **Physiological Researches on Life and Death.** 1827

Browne, Thomas. **Hydriotaphia.** 1927

Carrington, Hereward. **Death:** Its Causes and Phenomena with Special Reference to Immortality. 1921

Comper, Frances M. M., editor. **The Book of the Craft of Dying and Other Early English Tracts Concerning Death.** 1917

Death and the Visual Arts. 1976

Death as a Speculative Theme in Religious, Scientific, and Social Thought. 1976

Donne, John. **Biathanatos.** 1930

Farber, Maurice L. **Theory of Suicide.** 1968

Fechner, Gustav Theodor. **The Little Book of Life After Death.** 1904

Frazer, James George. **The Fear of the Dead in Primitive Religion.** Three vols. in one. 1933/1934/1936

Fulton, Robert. **A Bibliography on Death, Grief and Bereavement:** 1845-1975. 1976

Gorer, Geoffrey. **Death, Grief, and Mourning.** 1965

Gruman, Gerald J. **A History of Ideas About the Prolongation of Life.** 1966

Henry, Andrew F. and James F. Short, Jr. **Suicide and Homicide.** 1954

Howells, W[illiam] D[ean], et al. **In After Days;** Thoughts on the Future Life. 1910

Irion, Paul E. **The Funeral:** Vestige or Value? 1966

Landsberg, Paul-Louis. **The Experience of Death:** The Moral Problem of Suicide. 1953

Maeterlinck, Maurice. **Before the Great Silence.** 1937

Maeterlinck, Maurice. **Death.** 1912

Metchnikoff, Élie. **The Nature of Man:** Studies in Optimistic Philosophy. 1910

Metchnikoff, Élie. **The Prolongation of Life:** Optimistic Studies. 1908

Munk, William. **Euthanasia.** 1887

Osler, William. **Science and Immortality.** 1904

Return to Life: Two Imaginings of the Lazarus Theme. 1976

Stephens, C[harles] A[sbury]. **Natural Salvation:** The Message of Science. 1905

Sulzberger, Cyrus. **My Brother Death.** 1961

Taylor, Jeremy. **The Rule and Exercises of Holy Dying.** 1819

Walker, G[eorge] A[lfred]. **Gatherings from Graveyards.** 1839

Warthin, Aldred Scott. **The Physician of the Dance of Death.** 1931

Whiter, Walter. **Dissertation on the Disorder of Death.** 1819

Whyte, Florence. **The Dance of Death in Spain and Catalonia.** 1931

Wolfenstein, Martha. **Disaster:** A Psychological Essay. 1957

Worcester, Alfred. **The Care of the Aged, the Dying, and the Dead.** 1950

Zandee, J[an]. **Death as an Enemy According to Ancient Egyptian Conceptions.** 1960